Advance Praise for *Running for Our Lives*

"Robb Ryerse is the kind of guy who believes in big ideas that are daring enough that they just might happen. As I found in my travels across red-state Christian America, our country desperately needs those big ideas and the kind of people—like Robb— who are willing to risk it all with the hope that things might get better for us all. As a pastor, a journalist, and a parent, I find hope in knowing that Robb's story exists and that despite his electoral defeat, he hasn't stopped believing. We need more stories like Robb's in today's America, stories that prove some people do still get into politics hoping to make things better for someone other than themselves."
—ANGELA DENKER, author of *Red State Christians: Understanding the Voters Who Elected Donald Trump*

"A passionate, insightful, and skilled grassroots strategist, Robb Ryerse has given a gift to all politically conscious Americans. In *Running for Our Lives,* Robb therapeutically gives words to what so many of us felt deeply and painfully about the 2016 presidential election. This is not just a polemic, though; it's also a how-to manual when it comes to the existential question, What can we do? If you've been vexed by the turn in religious voting in America, you'll be relieved and encouraged after reading this book. We are not in a hopeless place—and Robb Ryerse doesn't just say it, but he proves it to us by what he and others have already done to steer us all on a better path toward a brighter tomorrow."
—ROB SCHENCK, president of the Dietrich Bonhoeffer Institute and author of *Costly Grace: An Evangelical Minister's Rediscovery of Faith, Hope, and Love*

"There is no time more important than now to talk about faith and politics. There is no person better than Robb Ryerse to lead us in that conversation. This book will be a crucial starting point for some, a provocative call for other ̱ ̱ ̱ ̱ ̱ ̱ ̱ ̱ ̱ ̱ ̱ of the journey for all of us on the engageme ̱ ̱ ̱ good."
Executive
ion Good

"I admire the courage of Rо̱ ̱ ̱ ̱ ̱ ̱ ̱ ̱ ve difficult conversations. So much of politics is poll-tested and consultant-driven, but Robb's commitment is the opposite: to run as a GOP progressive when Trump and the Tea Party are ascendant and to organize evangelicals to support Democrats, when, for so many, church and party are inextricably aligned. We need more voices like Robb's to expand the universe of what is possible as we build a stronger democracy."

—MIKE SIEGEL, **candidate for Texas's Tenth Congressional District**

"Terminal toxicity now defines the words *Christian, evangelical,* and *Republican.* For those (like me) who still hope for the good side of faith and Republicanism to reemerge based on grace and the common good, Robb Ryerse's *Running for Our Lives* offers real hope. If there's any way back to sanity for the Republican and religious faithful post-Trump, this book offers the road map."

—FRANK SCHAEFFER, **author of** *Crazy for God: How I Grew Up as One of the Elect, Helped Found the Religious Right, and Lived to Take All (or Almost All) of It Back*

"I got to know Robb as a Brand New Congress slatemate. I expected to meet someone I would disagree with a lot. Instead, I met an ally and the team encourager."

—CORI BUSH, **candidate for Missouri's First Congressional District and star of Netflix's** *Knock Down the House*

"I'm grateful that the Spirit is stirring women and men to engage in public life for the common good, through both U.S. political parties and as independents. Robb Ryerse may not have won his race in 2018, but he and many others have stepped up to shift the moral narrative in America. I'm grateful for him."

—JONATHAN WILSON-HARTGROVE, **author of** *Revolution of Values: Reclaiming Public Faith for the Common Good*

"It's likely that the only thing to save our divided and anxious country right now is courageous acts of love taken by brave people of grace. Thankfully, Robb Ryerse shows us how it's done. He and his wife, Vanessa, say yes to the ridiculous notion that extraordinary ordinary people—full of courage and love—are who our country needs right now to lead us. Sure, our political atmosphere feels hopeless at times, but Robb reminds me that as long as good people keep doing good work, there's always reason to hope."

—COLBY MARTIN, **author of** *UnClobber* **and** *The Shift*

"So much of modern politics is about bashing the other side or being against things. What I like about Robb is that he—and his message—brings people together."

—J. D. SCHOLTEN, **candidate for Iowa's Fourth Congressional District**

RUNNING
FOR OUR
LIVES

RUNNING
FOR OUR
LIVES

A Story of Faith, Politics,
and the Common Good

ROBB RYERSE

WESTMINSTER
JOHN KNOX PRESS
LOUISVILLE • KENTUCKY

© 2020 Robb Ryerse

First edition
Published by Westminster John Knox Press
Louisville, Kentucky

20 21 22 23 24 25 26 27 28 29 —10 9 8 7 6 5 4 3 2 1

Unless otherwise indicated, Scripture quotations are from the New Revised Standard Version of the Bible, copyright © 1989 by the Division of Christian Education of the National Council of the Churches of Christ in the U.S.A., and are used by permission.

Book design by Drew Stevens
Cover design by Nita Ybarra

Library of Congress Cataloging-in-Publication Data is on file at the Library of Congress, Washington, DC.

ISBN-13: 978-0-664-26621-9

Most Westminster John Knox Press books are available at special quantity discounts when purchased in bulk by corporations, organizations, and special-interest groups. For more information, please e-mail SpecialSales@wjkbooks.com.

I ran for
Matt, Calvin, Charleigh, and Whimsy

Contents

Foreword

You know how you meet some people who make a great first impression, and the more you get to know them, the more the luster wears off? And you know how you meet other people, and the longer you know them, the more impressed you are with them?

You're about to read the story of one of the latter kinds of people. The story of how Robb and I met is kind of funny.

Here's how I remember it: I was settling in for a red-eye from California home to Florida, via Atlanta (of course), in the cheap seats, of course. Ear buds in, a pillow positioned against the window, I was just drifting off as a fellow came down the aisle and caught my tired eye.

"You!" he pointed at me. "You're Brian McLaren! I've read all your books!"

Then he looked at the poor fellow in the middle seat next to me. "Can I trade seats with you?" Robb asked. "This guy's books really helped me, and I'd love to talk to him."

"No," the fellow answered flatly, with no reason beyond that. (If Robb had offered him an aisle seat, it might have been different.)

I stepped in. "I'll wait for you on the jetway in Atlanta," I said to this enthusiastic fellow. "If you have time, we can get breakfast." Robb smiled, gave me a thumbs-up, and moved on to his seat even farther back than mine.

The fellow next to me said, "I don't know who you are, but I think you owe me one."

We both laughed, and I proceeded to try to fall asleep in the cheap seats. Through taxi, takeoff, ascent, cruising altitude, and descent, I only succeeded in discovering new ways to be uncomfortable.

After landing, I waited on the jetway in Atlanta, met Robb, and over breakfast we became friends. What was not to like about a guy brimming with this much enthusiasm, creativity, sincerity, intelligence, and chutzpah?

In the coming years, I had the opportunity to visit the church he and his wife, Vanessa, had planted. I also got to read and enthusiastically endorse his first book, *Fundamorphosis*.

In early 2017, when I heard he was running for Congress, I thought, *Of course.*

Robb's decision made perfect sense to me because I understood that his theology was not about escaping earth and going to heaven, but rather, it was about God's kingdom coming to earth, God's will being done on earth. His creative work as a pastor was dedicated to that end, and his work as a politician would be similar—not as a theocrat of any sort, but as a person who would sincerely seek the good of all his constituents, whether they were Christian, Muslim, Jewish, atheist, agnostic, whatever.

Rather than being driven by a partisan ideology of the right or left, I knew Robb was driven by the common good, and I felt that he was exactly the kind of person our country needs in office these days, whatever their religion, whatever their party, and whatever the office.

I won't spoil the story by telling you how Robb won (or not), nor will I tell you his party affiliation or platform (you'll find out soon, and you'll be surprised). But I will say that reading this book not only deepened my appreciation for Robb, it helped restore my hope in democracy.

I don't think I'm the only one who needs my hope restored.

I can't help but remember another friend of mine who ran for Congress many years ago. After he lost, I asked what he felt went wrong, and he said, "One thing makes it fundamentally impossible for me to win political office: my deep and abiding distrust in the American people."

My concerns about democracy are less about distrust in the American people (although sometimes there's that too) and more about the outsized role that money plays in politics. The rich, it has become abundantly clear, are much more equal than others—and as a result, we now have the best democracy that money can buy, but not government "of the people, by the people, and for the people."

Robb's story gave me hope that "extraordinary ordinary people" can get in the game and make a difference. True, they're the exception these days, but if enough of us vote for long enough, we could turn the tide.

We all have reasons to be disgusted about the slow dance that religion and politics typically engage in during these times, cheek to cheek and chest to chest, whispering adoring love talk into one another's ears, both swaying to the band of big donors who are calling the tune and choosing the rhythm.

But in this book, you'll see a very different vision of religion and politics, especially in regard to the common good. Instead of a sleazy dance, you'll see a vision of vigorous conversation, mutual challenge, and, when possible, intelligent collaboration. You'll see a kind of religion that imagines a better kind of politics, and a kind of politics that prays for a better kind of religion.

I don't know what the future holds for Robb, but I do know this: he hasn't been the same since embarking on his campaign for Congress. He has seen behind the curtain, so to speak, and now he sees within a bigger frame. I suspect that if you read his book with an open mind and heart, the same will happen for you.

And that will be a big win—for Robb, for you, and for us all.

Brian D. McLaren
August 2019

Introduction

This story begins on Election Day 2016.

Like millions of other Americans, I was sitting on my couch watching returns trickle in as polls closed in various states. Like millions of other Americans, I expected it to be an early night with a predictable result. I thought we'd be electing our first female president and that the reality TV star would parlay his time in the political spotlight into his own television network. Like millions of other Americans, I was not prepared for what actually happened.

When Pennsylvania was called for Donald Trump, I poured myself a drink. My son Calvin and I did the math on remaining states and chatted about how it was going to end up much closer than we had anticipated. When the networks called Ohio and Michigan, it became obvious that Donald Trump was going to win the Electoral College.

About that time, my wife, Vanessa, came into the living room and shared with me some other news. That morning, a dear friend of ours had suddenly lost his infant son. She didn't have many details, but my heart and mind immediately went to my friend Alan, an extraordinary dad whose pain, I imagined, was beyond anything I could bear.

I began to weep. I cried for a long time that night. I cried uncontrollably. When I think back on it, part of me wants to blame the whiskey, but the truth is I cried because of the deep pain I felt.

I wept for Alan and his family.

I wept for Hillary Clinton.

I wept for America.

I woke up the following day with a deep sense that I had to do something. What had taken place the night before was so unexpected, so disconcerting, so destabilizing to me that I knew inaction was no longer an option.

My first priority was to give space for the women in my life to grieve. Not only had America not elected its first female president, we had, in fact, elected a man who bragged about his mistreatment of women. Vanessa invited her friends over to lament together. I stayed quiet on social media and in person, listening first to their stories and grief.

In the ensuing days, I began engaging in conversations with friends about how they felt. It was as if I was having the same exchange over and over again.

"I just can't believe this."

"I know. I feel like we have to do something, like *I* have to do something."

"I feel the same way. What are you going to do?"

"I'm not sure."

"Well, I'm getting involved."

And my friends did get involved. They started attending protests and rallies. They began writing letters to their senators and representatives. They organized with groups like Indivisible, Moms Demand Action, and Our Revolution. It was exhilarating to watch.

But I still wasn't sure what I was supposed to do, how I was supposed to be involved. I just didn't know what the election of Donald Trump was going to mean for me personally or what action I was going to take. Each day as I watched the news, feeling utterly dumbfounded, I grew increasingly convinced that I was going to have some part to play in the unfolding drama of it all. But I could not even imagine what that would be. So I committed myself to listening and waiting until the universe made it clear.

That happened on Inauguration Day.

1

You've Got to Do This

★ ★ ★

Rethinking My Call
to Ministry and the Gospel

On January 20, 2017, Inauguration Day, I got up and went to work like it was any other day. I decided not to watch any of the pomp and circumstance. I still hadn't made peace with the fact that Donald Trump was going to be our president, and I just didn't want to see it come to pass.

My wife, Vanessa, feeling much the same way, avoided the television but at some point listened to a podcast, strategically timed for Inauguration Day. It was Rob Bell's *RobCast*, and his guest was Zack Exley, the founder of a new organization called Brand New Congress.

Zack explained to Rob that a lot of energy and resources get devoted to who we elect as president, and that's good and important. However, who represents us in the halls of Congress is equally important, but it doesn't get nearly the same attention. In fact, Congress has an abysmal approval rating and yet incumbents enjoy a reelection rate of over 90 percent.

What would happen, Zack dreamed, if hundreds of regular, everyday Americans ran for Congress, challenging the entrenched incumbents in both parties, swearing off donations from corporations and their lobbyists, and having a unified set of proposals for actually solving the biggest problems we face as a country? Could we change the country in a truly revolutionary way?

5

He used a word he had coined: "postpartisan." The idea of Brand New Congress was to get beyond the typical partisan divide of American politics by running Republicans in bright-red districts and Democrats in deep blue districts. Candidates were in different parties but on the same team. The idea was brilliantly subversive. And it resonated with Vanessa.

When Vanessa and I had started our church, Vintage Fellowship in Fayetteville, Arkansas, more than a decade before, we began referring to it as "postdenominational." Just like "bipartisan" has become pretty meaningless in politics, we always felt like "nondenominational" was a bland description of what we were trying to do. I think our use of "postdenominational" made Vanessa particularly receptive to Zack's postpartisan vision.

When I walked through the door that evening, Vanessa held her phone out at me. "You've got to listen to this," she said. "You've got to do this."

Vanessa and I often recommend books and podcasts to each other. I guess over the years, we've developed an unspoken understanding that neither one of us is really obligated to read or listen to whatever the other is recommending. But her earnestness about this particular podcast made me think something was different this time.

That evening, after the kids had gone to bed, I opened up the podcast app on my phone and gave this particular *RobCast* a listen. I was sold. I drank the Kool-Aid.

I had woken up that day thinking it was a normal day. I went to bed that night thinking I might run for Congress.

The next day, I listened to it again. And then I began calling friends and telling them to listen too. I had lunch with others I knew were *RobCast* regulars to get their impressions of Zack's big idea. People were intrigued. And so was I.

I told them that I "wouldn't be opposed" to them nominating me as a Brand New Congress candidate. I guess several of them did nominate me, because about a week later, I was sitting on my back porch enjoying a cigar with a friend when my phone rang.

"Robb, I'm from Brand New Congress. You've been nominated to run for Congress. We'd like to talk to you about it. Are you free tomorrow for an in-depth conversation?"

I said yes.

Saying yes to this unlikely and somewhat bizarre idea was pretty significant for me. I had long ago abandoned my political dreams, but they were now resurfacing.

I grew up a political junkie, and a conservative one at that. When I was fifteen years old, I had two magazine subscriptions: *Sports Illustrated* and *National Review*. I read Barry Goldwater books. I had signed headshots of Senators Bob Dole and Alfonse D'Amato and Congressman Newt Gingrich hanging on my bedroom wall. One summer, I attended Teenage Republican School in Albany, New York. When I was sixteen, I skipped school to call in to Rush Limbaugh's radio show and actually made it on the air!

Long before the days of cell phones, on election nights I would ride my bike from the county courthouse back to the Republican Party gathering to report results from precincts. I proudly wore my "God is Pro-Life" T-shirt and attended the March for Life in Washington, DC.

For the school science fair my sophomore year of high school, I wrote a basic computer program that allowed the user to enter any year and learn about who was president at that time, along with a description of his accomplishments. For my own amusement, I built the program so that if you entered "2013," the first year I would be eligible to be president, it would describe my presidency.

All I wanted to do was to go into politics. Everything about it fascinated me.

Instead, my priorities were upended by my matriculation at the small, fundamentalist Baptist Bible college that my parents and my sisters had attended. Our denomination was birthed in the conflict between modernism and fundamentalism in the early 1900s. Pastors and seminary professors fought over the inspiration of the Bible, the miracles and resurrection of Jesus, and many other things they thought were at the core of our faith.

One of the main points of conflict was over the nature of the gospel. I was taught in church and Bible college that the true message of the gospel centered on the salvation of the souls of individuals. Modernists and liberals, I was warned, watered down this message with a "social gospel" about meeting the felt needs of people. A Christian who focused on making sure people were educated or lifted out of poverty would be missing their biggest need: to be saved from their sins. If we were to help people in any way, it was only as a means of being able to share with them the true gospel of eternal salvation.

This understanding of the gospel coincided with a view of the end of the world that we also learned. Dispensationalism, as it is known, downplayed cultural and social involvement and emphasized the work of getting people "saved." There was no need to recycle or worry about the environment, for instance, when the Rapture was going to happen at any moment. Our first priority was to get as many people as possible to accept Jesus as their Lord and Savior so that they could go to heaven. We had to constantly be aware of the slippery slope that would move us away from the true gospel. While it was probably acceptable to protest abortion, we were taught to be very leery of other political involvement because it would distract us from our primary mission of saving people. Consequently, a deep divide opened between the sacred and the secular, between the church and the world. Politics and all of its social concern was secular, earthly, worldly, temporal. The work of the church was sacred and eternal.

During the fall of my freshman year of college, we had a weeklong Bible conference in which a preacher from Michigan spoke a sentence that cut me to the heart. He bellowed, "If God calls you to be a pastor, you'd have to stoop to be a king."

In that moment, I was convinced that my political ambitions were holding me back from what I should be doing, what

God wanted me to do, namely, to be a pastor. I still wanted to change the world for the better; I just came to believe that the best way to do so was by investing myself in church leadership because the church was God's chosen method of bringing salvation to the world. From then on, I would refer to that sermon as my "call to ministry." That was the moment in which I committed myself to be a pastor and to surrender my dream of being a politician. The path of my life was set.

Near the end of that school year, one of our professors arranged for a group of us to take a field trip to Washington, DC. If we set up a meeting with our congressperson during the trip and wrote a summary, we could avoid writing a lengthy term paper. So, I scheduled a meeting with my congressman, a moderate Republican named Sherwood Boehlert. Congressman Boehlert and I had a nice conversation, and at the end of it, he suggested I join his staff. A few weeks later, I received a letter from his office offering me a summer internship that could lead to much more.

It truly was a fork-in-the-road moment for me. I could move to DC and get started in politics like I had always dreamed, or I could continue my studies at Bible college and become a pastor. There was really no decision to make. God had called me to be a pastor.

Three years later, I graduated, married my sweetheart, and began my first pastoral ministry at a small church at the very southern tip of Staten Island in New York City. A few months later, I was ordained and began working on my seminary degree. I was called to be a minister of the gospel, and nothing else mattered.

My pastoral ministry did not go as I imagined it would.

I spent the next decade serving in conservative Baptist churches, rehearsing what I had been taught in Bible college, trying to make a name for myself in our denomination and build the life to which I thought God had called me.

But my foundations began to crack. In time, the answers I had been given stopped making sense. My experiences slowly changed my perspective, and I found myself asking questions that shook the core of my faith. I woke up on my thirtieth birthday deeply depressed and in a dark night of the soul.

I remember preparing to do a sermon series through the book of Genesis. For the first time in my life, I was seeing things differently. I asked myself questions like, "Why do the voices in Genesis 1 and Genesis 2 sound so different from one another? Are these chapters describing two different things? And doesn't Genesis 1 sound a lot more like poetry than history?" I knew that if I suggested these ideas to my fundamentalist congregation, I would be fired as their pastor.

I also started to have second thoughts about other things, like the doctrine of hell, for instance. One day, I was having lunch with a pastor friend of my mine and asked him, "Wouldn't it be just like God to surprise us with grace and let everyone into heaven?" He was shocked by my question and tried to convince me otherwise, but I wasn't so sure.

My questions weren't just theological. They were also methodological. Did this sharp distinction between the church and the world really make sense? Shouldn't we care about the physical, psychological, and material needs of people as much as we care about their spiritual needs? What would church look like if it existed to serve people instead of save people? What if the slippery-slope argument was just a scare tactic designed to indoctrinate us?

The reality of my questions weighed heavily on me, and I came to realize that, in good conscience, I couldn't continue to pastor like I had in the past. I also knew that if I was going to explore these ideas publicly, I would end up splitting my fundamentalist congregation.

All of this was taking place in a time when the "emergent church" was becoming a popular idea in evangelical Christianity. I started reading authors like Brian McLaren, Doug Pagitt, and Rob Bell. I was starting to see that I could be a pastor who was honest about my questions and doubts; I just wasn't going to be able to do that in our particular denomination.

After much discussion and planning, Vanessa and I decided

to leave behind pretty much everyone and everything we had ever known. We packed up all of our earthly possessions and moved halfway across the country to Northwest Arkansas to start a new church. Vintage Fellowship was born in 2006, a self-described emergent church that would be a safe place for people who had left the certainty of fundamentalism, who had bad church experiences elsewhere, and who needed a big theological yard to play in. Vanessa and I were fond of saying, "We have to pastor a church we would go to even if they weren't paying us to be there."

Vintage became a place where we actively, holistically tried to meet people's needs. Rather than just caring about people's spiritual needs, we recognized that their mental, physical, psychological, and economic needs are important too. It was a community where people from different denominational backgrounds and perspectives came together to listen to and learn from each other. Eventually, we clarified, too, that Vintage was a place where everyone was welcome, regardless of their sexual orientation or gender identity.

It was—and still is—my favorite church ever.

This transformation, or "fundamorphosis" as I began to call it, profoundly changed me. It prepared me to realize that what I thought was two different paths—the "religious" and the "secular"—were actually one and the same. My life as a pastor, leading a church community, was really no different than any other part of my life. Being involved in politics could be a vital expression of my commitments to see divine love, peace, and justice extended to all people. The gospel to which I was called to be a minister was actually big enough to be good news for all aspects of every person's life.

One story from the life of Jesus brought this into clear focus for me. Jesus and his disciples were walking one day and saw a man begging on the side of the road, a man who had been born blind. The disciples took this opportunity to ask Jesus a gossipy question: "Who sinned, this man or his parents, that he was born blind?"

The question betrayed a common belief at the time that sickness was the result of sin. If someone had a debilitating disease of some kind, someone was responsible for it. Maybe his parents had done something that caused the blindness. Maybe the man himself had sinned in some way, bringing on the ailment. Either way, the man was sick, and it was his or his family's fault.

Good news for the man born blind wasn't a question of whose sin needed to be forgiven. Good news for him was his physical need being addressed so that he could stop begging and not have to live in poverty any longer.

Jesus rebuffed his disciples' question, refusing to place blame on the man or his parents. He met the man's need and healed him of his blindness. The gospel that Jesus brought to people was good news for their whole selves.

But this story has even more to say about how we engage in politics.

When we read this now, we probably think, "Aren't Jesus' disciples so quaint?" We look back with bemusement that people would think that someone's health was directly tied to their character. Do the right thing and be healthy. Do the wrong thing and be sick. We know now that it's just not that straightforward and simple. Or do we?

During the debate in 2017 about a proposed plan to repeal and replace the Affordable Care Act, a Republican congressman went on a news program and suggested that people who cannot afford health insurance are in that position because they've probably foolishly spent their money on a new iPhone.

This comment betrays a common belief of our time, that poor people can't afford health insurance because they have sinned. Whether many people would say it outright or not, they believe that people are poor because they lack discipline, they are lazy, or they don't have enough faith. Sin is the cause.

It is not uncommon to hear people who receive government assistance disparaged in sermons in fundamentalist and evangelical churches: "The Bible clearly says, 'If you don't work, you don't eat.'" Obviously, someone who would be so foolish as to buy a new iPhone rather than health insurance has sinful priorities or some kind of character deficiency. Who sinned that you don't have health care? It's either your fault or your family's.

But Jesus did not treat the man this way. He didn't blame a poor person for being in need. Poverty, then and now, is far more complicated an issue. Generational poverty, income inequality, rural underdevelopment, and lack of access to education and opportunity are all much more likely reasons for someone to be unable to pay health insurance premiums. Not being able to afford health care is not a sin problem. Jesus didn't judge people needing health care, so neither should we.

He didn't lecture the man about how he needed to take "personal responsibility," as many conservative Christians today tend to do. Instead, Jesus took responsibility for the man's health care. He did what he could to meet the man's needs.

This story is no anomaly. Over and over again throughout the Gospels, Jesus didn't just meet people's spiritual needs. He treated the whole person. He spoke out against those who used their power to oppress and marginalize people. He welcomed people of different ethnicities. He consistently identified with the poor and needy.

The gospel of Jesus is not just spiritual good news; it is social good news too. The gospel may not be partisan, but it is unquestionably political.

One of the ways Vintage Fellowship experimented with this understanding of the gospel was to welcome a refugee family. A new organization had started in our area called Canopy Northwest Arkansas. Its mission was to live out faith in the gospel by helping to resettle refugees from war-torn parts of the world. When we learned of the work Canopy was doing, we decided to get involved.

Our congregation formed a team and started to put into place everything needed to help a family move to our community. For months, this team raised money, learned about different cultures, downloaded translation apps to their phones, and prepared a home for our soon-to-be neighbors. Eventually, a mother and her four children arrived, and we welcomed them.

They were Iraqi refugees, a Muslim family. And we wanted them to feel loved, with no strings attached.

This experience reinforced for me the reality that the fear-mongering messages we often receive from the media have little basis in the truth. We're told that Muslim refugees ought to be banned from entering our country because they are probably just terrorists in disguise. The people I met did not fit this stereotype. They were good people, just like everyone else, trying to make a better life for themselves and their children. I was happy to have them in our community and proud of the work Vintage did to welcome them.

But not everyone felt that way. In fact, our congressman, Representative Steve Womack, wrote a letter to then–secretary of state John Kerry urging him to decertify Canopy as a refugee resettlement agency, effectively ending the work done by people like those in my own congregation. I was outraged by this letter.

The gospel is about more than just converting people to our religion. It's about meeting the needs of people, especially those people who are in very vulnerable situations. *How could someone who claimed, as Womack did, to follow the ways of Jesus fail to see that helping refugee families is what the gospel is all about?* I wondered.

I had voted for him in the past, but in November 2016 I couldn't vote again for a man who was directly opposed to the good work being done by good people in our community and in my church. Thankfully his request was denied, but still I thought, *Someone has to run against him.*

When Brand New Congress called, I knew that I was going to be that person.

2

Congress Camp

★ ★ ★

Coming Together
for a Common Purpose

The first couple months of 2017 were a whirlwind of activity. Brand New Congress had a training regimen developed for nominees that covered the gamut of things a candidate for Congress would need to consider. I did self-guided lessons on crafting my personal story, responding to the press, and understanding policy positions. I even had to lock down my personal Internet security by changing all my passwords. As a first-time political candidate, I was so thankful to have a road map to follow.

I was also thankful for the input of trusted people around me. I spent hours talking with family and friends about whether running for Congress was actually a good idea or not. Before I committed to this major decision, I sought the wisdom of people who knew me well. As I described what I was considering, most had a similar reaction—a mix of amusement at the audacity of the idea; concerns about how I would juggle family, church, and my day job with campaigning; and genuine offers of support and help should I decide to go forward.

One friend in particular, a veteran of politics in my home state of Arkansas, was the outlier. He tried to talk me out of it. He came prepared with three pages of notes about why this idea would never work. He urged me to consider, given my views on issues such as health care and LGBTQIA protections, how out of step I was with many other Arkansas Republican voters. He said I'd never be able to raise enough money to be successful. He told me my platform was nowhere near big enough to mount an effective campaign. Besides, he said, I wouldn't really even like the job of being a congressman. He probably didn't know it, but he was actually echoing the script that was already running in my head about why it was foolish for me to entertain the idea of running for Congress.

Nonetheless, I could not shake the compelling sense that the Trump administration and its cohorts in Congress posed a significant threat to the future of the country. The attempts of leaders in Washington to repeal the Affordable Care Act in the early part of 2017 served as the counternarrative to my doubts. They weren't just debating inconsequential policy positions, I told myself; they were putting people's lives at risk. Posting my dissent on Facebook was simply not enough anymore. I woke up every day feeling like I had to do something. The opportunity that had unexpectedly presented itself to me was a congressional campaign, and so, despite all the good and rational reasons not to, I kept taking steps toward running.

One of those steps included attending a town hall that Representative Womack held in Harrison, Arkansas. My friend Scott and I went together, wanting to see for ourselves if Womack warranted a challenger to his seat. The local branches of grassroots advocacy network Indivisible had mobilized, and the crowd was not a friendly one for the congressman. He did not, however, listen to questions sincerely and answer questions respectfully. In all of my life, I had never seen a person be so rude to an audience.

Halfway through, I leaned over to Scott and whispered, "Am I just seeing what I want to see? Am I imagining how badly this is going?"

"No. You're not imagining anything. It's that bad," Scott replied.

As we left the auditorium that night, I said to Scott, "Somebody's got to beat that guy."

"It might as well be you," Scott said, winking at me.

We decided to take the next big step of attending what Vanessa lovingly dubbed "Congress Camp."

In junior high school, I spent my summers at church camp. In high school and even into college, I worked at camp. I loved living in a cabin, eating suspicious camp food, playing unique camp games, and hearing campers tell their stories of transformation around the end-of-the-week bonfire. Some of the bonds I made at church camp remain strong to this day.

So, in April when Brand New Congress invited me and four other possible congressional candidates to visit their headquarters in Knoxville, Tennessee, for candidate training. I was in.

Our days were packed with activities that mirrored the energy and excitement I used to experience at church camp. We practiced our stump speeches for one another. We taped and reviewed mock interviews with major media outlets. We were schooled on the ins and outs of setting up a campaign team. We deepened our grasp of the viability of what we each were about to undertake.

Most of all, we bonded.

None of us had ever run for office. We had all been nominated for this adventure and recruited by Brand New Congress. As political newbies, we probably wouldn't strike fear in the hearts of Washington insiders, but we were united by our desire to do something to change the course on which our country found itself. The Brand New Congress leadership called us "extraordinary ordinary Americans," a phrase that gave me hope every time it was repeated.

Undeniably, we were an eclectic group of potential candidates.

Paula Jean Swearengin, a coal miner's daughter a couple years older than me, was planning on running for the U.S. Senate from West Virginia. Her opponent in the Democratic primary would be Senator Joe Manchin. I knew immediately that Paula Jean was going to be a formidable candidate because of her ability to stay on message. She tied every single conversation we had back to how families in West Virginia were suffering and even dying because of the actions of the coal industry and the elected officials it bought and paid for with campaign donations. Tears would well up in her eyes. She struck me as a passionate and powerful advocate.

Sarah Smith, a redheaded millennial from Seattle, Washington, displayed an encyclopedic knowledge of the issues. I didn't know anything about her primary opponent, Congressman Adam Smith, before I met Sarah, but I sensed that he was going to have his hands full if he and Sarah ever debated. A few months later, when I watched the live stream of a debate between the two Smiths from Seattle, I was not surprised that Sarah ran circles around him. She was so persuasive in her arguments that he ultimately was forced to adopt many of her positions in the general election.

Michael Hepburn, a young African American man from South Florida, consistently made me smile with his enthusiasm and what he called his "new perspective." He told us stories of taking public transportation from his place of employment to the neighborhoods he was canvassing in the evenings. I wondered how far behind I was if he was already out campaigning. In the middle of Congress Camp, Michael got a phone call; his opponent unexpectedly announced that she was retiring. He speculated, correctly as it turned out, that his race would attract some big-name competitors, even a former Clinton administration cabinet secretary.

The final member of our cohort was a young Latina from the Bronx. She told us about her nonprofit work, her day job as a bartender, and how she was going to be challenging the fourth-ranking Democrat in the House of Representatives, Joe Crowley. She possessed a charisma that was infectious. I wanted to hear more about her take on just about every subject. She spoke clearly, compellingly, and with conviction. In fact, when I got home from Congress Camp, I told Vanessa that I had met someone I thought could end up as president of the United States someday. Her name was Alexandria Ocasio-Cortez.

The five of us, along with the Brand New Congress team, spent the weekend talking about what is wrong in our political system. But more than that, we also talked about what we could do to fix it. We imagined how we as regular people could run campaigns that didn't rely on the corrupting influence of corporate donations. We schemed about subverting a system that most benefits incumbents and the political party establishments.

We also talked about issues that typically divide Americans. Nothing was off limits. We discussed if it is possible to bring pro-choice and pro-life voters together. We crafted arguments to convince small-government conservatives to support a revamping of our health-care system through a policy of Medicare for All. We bemoaned how the only thing that seems to unite congresspeople from both sides of the aisle is their love for military spending. The conversations were enlightening and electric.

We didn't always agree, but we listened to each other. We tried to understand each others' viewpoints. Even though we came from such different backgrounds, locations, and perspectives, we found common ground on which we could agree, always being mindful of what it would take to win in our respective districts. This weekend of conversation demonstrated something very important to me. Despite the fact we're repeatedly told that American society is at an impasse—that we are more divided than ever by party and identity—there is actually a path forward.

"Identity politics" is the term used to describe the segmentation of people into separate groups and the attempt to appeal to them on issues about which they uniquely care. Instead of trying to build consensus by appealing to a broad swath of voters, those who practice identity politics are constantly slicing and dicing the electorate, tailoring their message to their targets. Both political parties use identity politics to keep their bases of support energized. Campaigns often pit groups against each other based on demographics they deem important: rural, urban, or suburban; black, Hispanic, or white; men or women; religious or nonreligious; and so on.

In his book *Identity*, Francis Fukuyama describes how this approach to politics has played out over the past one hundred years in America:

> Twentieth-century politics had been organized along a left-right spectrum defined by economic issues, the left wanting more equality and the right demanding greater freedom. Progressive politics centered around workers, their trade unions, and social democratic parties that sought better social protections and economic redistribution. The right by contrast was primarily interested in reducing the size of government and promoting the private sector. In the second decade of the twenty-first century, that spectrum appears to be giving way in many regions to one defined by identity. The left has focused less on broad economic equality and more on promoting the interests of a wide variety of groups perceived as being marginalized—blacks, immigrants, women, Hispanics, the LGBT community, refugees, and the like. The right, meanwhile, is redefining itself as patriots who seek to protect traditional national identity, an identity that is often explicitly connected to race, ethnicity, or religion.[1]

Though common, one of the weaknesses of this approach is that it oversimplifies complex issues. Instead of speaking honestly about how complicated the problems we face are, politicians develop platitudes that serve as dog whistles to intended audiences. Further, identity politics has a tendency to marginalize people who don't fit neatly into one of the demographic groups. People, like the issues, are far more complex than politicians and their messaging consultants recognize.

While it may be an effective political tool, the broad embrace and employment of identity politics has had a negative impact on our system. Most significantly, identity politics reinforces tribalism.

It is human nature to find one's identity in a tribe. Nothing is inherently wrong with this; in fact, it can reinforce a sense of belonging and community. I was born in Cleveland, Ohio, and spent my elementary years there, so I am a lifelong and avid fan of the Cleveland Browns. It can be kind of lonely being a Browns fan in Arkansas. On Christmas vacation one year, our family attended a game at Cleveland Browns Stadium. We parked and headed toward the field. As we crested a hill, we saw a sea of brown and orange as tens of thousands of other fans made their way into the stadium. My eldest child, who was ten years old at the time, looked up at me and said, "Dad, we're not the only ones."

Being a part of a tribe is not a bad thing. But when our identities cause us to turn against, distrust, and refuse to cooperate with one another, tribalism becomes a real danger.

I've observed this kind of tribalism throughout my time as a pastor. People's primary loyalty is to their church or their denomination. They are suspicious of others who don't belong to their group. It can be notoriously difficult to get local churches to work together on a project that would benefit their community because some are concerned about who will get the credit while others want to invest only in the ministries of their particular congregation. I've often joked that the fundamentalist Baptist denomination in which I grew up didn't necessarily believe we were the only ones who were going to heaven, but they definitely thought we would be on the first bus.

Tribalism has become a staple of American politics. The Republican and Democratic Parties are both so invested in their own victory that they are unable to compromise or cooperate. Many of the people who identify with one of the major political parties can't conceive of how their friends or family would be part of the other tribe. The competition of politics transforms into a type of warfare in which destroying your opponent is the most acceptable outcome. Civility becomes passé.

A stark example of this played out in 2016. When Supreme Court Justice Antonin Scalia unexpectedly passed away, President Barack Obama nominated Merrick Garland to replace him. At any other time in history, Judge Garland would have flown through the confirmation hearings in the Senate. He was a consensus pick whom everyone expected to be a moderate voice on the Court.

However, Republicans in the Senate did not want to give President Obama the opportunity to name another Supreme Court Justice who would serve a lifetime appointment, likely tipping the balance of the Court away from conservatives, so they stonewalled. Led by Senate Majority Leader Mitch McConnell, they simply refused to give Judge Garland a hearing. Even though they were constitutionally required to do so, they just refused. Republicans proudly campaigned on their obstruction, assuring those who identify as religious pro-life voters that if elected, they would deliver a victory on this one issue. Once Donald Trump was elected, the Senate confirmed his pick, Neil Gorsuch, to the Court, scoring a major win for Republicans.

Tribalism won out over duty. A short-term victory was won, but the long-term effect of the Republicans' strategy is a deeper divide between the parties and an accompanying distrust of one another. Now that the precedent has been set, a constitutional crisis may be in our future should the same situation present itself again.

Republicans are not the only ones to blame. This same tribalism can be seen on the other side of the aisle as well. Throughout the 2018 midterms, many Democratic voters took to social media with the cry of #BlueNoMatterWho. Regardless of policy positions, personal character, or relevant experience, these voters were committed to cast their ballot solely based on the "D" after someone's name. The tribe trumped all else.

We can already see the fruit of this kind of partisan tribalism in our society, and, if left unchecked, it will continue to grow. It will entrench us in silos of suspicion and stifle conversation. It will cause us to stereotype each other based on party affiliation. We will consistently put party ahead of people, and then we will continue to wonder why our leaders can't work together to solve the biggest problems we face as a nation.

The experiment of Congress Camp called into question this long-established conventional wisdom and began to chart a new path. Could Republicans and Democrats sit down around a table and talk charitably and productively about real issues? Could people of different ethnicities, generations, and backgrounds hear one another's concerns and perspectives? Could we as potential candidates for Congress demonstrate that people are more important than party?

On the final day of Congress Camp, I sat at a folding table next to Alexandria Ocasio-Cortez as we filled out Federal Election Commission paperwork to begin our campaigns for Congress. We could not have been more different: a white Generation-X pastor from Arkansas and a millennial Latina waitress from New York City. I was from a bright-red, rural district in the South; she came from a densely populated, deep-blue district in the Northeast. A Republican and a Democrat.

We were from different tribes, but we were on the same team.

The trust we developed that weekend in Knoxville carried on throughout our campaigns. We rooted for one another. We encouraged each other through the difficulties of running for office. We shared resources and ideas that would make us more effective on the campaign trail. We celebrated our victories together and cried together in our defeats. We believed in each other.

I realized at Congress Camp that conversation can overcome tribalism. There is no substitute for sitting together and hearing other people's stories. Honest and authentic dialog opens us up to see the world differently. It's when we talk together that we remember that most of us are not the worst stereotypes of our tribe. Instead, we are people who are most often searching for solutions to the common challenges we face. Our journeys may have taken us on different directions in the past, but when we truly listen to one another, we find that we can apply to our own experiences the lessons others have learned.

When employed with authenticity and empathy, conversation builds trust. So much of the current American political divide is predicated upon suspicion and distrust. But it's hard to mischaracterize a person whose story I know and whose struggles I've heard. I can't assume the worst about someone with whom I've shared vulnerably. I can't dismiss someone with whom I've made a connection. The relationships cultivated in the soil of conversation can grow into meaningful connection.

This is one of the reasons I am a follower of Jesus. He exemplified this kind of connection. Every time I read John's Gospel, I am struck by the series of conversations Jesus had with people. He talked to Nicodemus, a rich and religious man of privilege and power. Jesus answered his questions and challenged his reality. He talked to the Samaritan woman at the well, a marginalized seeker who responded to his engagement. He talked to a paralyzed man whose only hope was superstitious folklore about the healing properties of the waters of a local pond. He talked to the crowds of people who were looking for someone who would deliver on their promises that their needs would be met.

In each of these interactions, Jesus demonstrated that the things that divide us can be overcome through authentic connection. Because he talked to them, people trusted Jesus. They believed in him.

When we talk to one another, we can learn to believe in one another as well.

Those who are cynical about American politics are convinced that the tribalism of the two-party system can't be overcome. They frequently complain that their elected officials won't cross the aisle to compromise. But how can we expect our leaders to put people ahead of party if we're unwilling to do it first? Congress Camp disabused me of my own cynicism and prompted a rebirth of hope.

3

Christian and Candidate

★ ★ ★

Questions at the Intersection
of Church and State

I returned home from Congress Camp in Knoxville more confident than ever that I was going to launch my congressional campaign. But there were a few other people whose support I knew I would need if I was going to take this leap.

The first and most critical conversation was with Vanessa. Throughout our marriage, we have always resisted new adventures if both of us were not completely sold on the idea. Because Vanessa had first learned of Brand New Congress and even suggested my run, I knew that I wouldn't have to sell her on the idea. But we still had to talk about how this would impact our lives. Would it be acceptable for me to be away from home at campaign events for so many evenings? Were we ready to take our family into the public square with the criticism that could come along with that? And, if by some crazy chance I won, were we prepared to live with me spending a lot of time in Washington, DC?

Looking back over our life together, Vanessa and I realized that we were less risk-averse than we had ever imagined. We made note of all of the risks we had taken—pastoring a small church in New York City right out of Bible college, leaving behind everything we had ever known to start a church in Arkansas, working for ourselves or for start-ups to make ends meet. Over and over again, we could see that the risks we had taken didn't make us rich and famous, but they had turned out to be pivotal steps in our journey. This risk would be no different, we assured ourselves. Ultimately, the things that motivated us to consider this idea in the first place proved to be weightier than the inconveniences we imagined. Our sense that someone had to step forward to publicly oppose the direction the Trump administration was taking the Republican Party and the country was unshaken. The road forward had presented itself to us. We decided to keep moving. Green light.

The next conversation was with our kids. We have four children, at the time two high schoolers, a junior high student, and a toddler who was our surprise baby. We tried to communicate to them the possible ramifications of my campaign for our family. They were as supportive as they could be. Green light.

I also needed to talk to my boss. Since we started Vintage Fellowship, I have been a bivocational pastor, working full-time to pay the bills while pastoring the church on the side. At that point, I worked for a Canadian-based start-up company. I worked from home with little oversight of my day-to-day activities. I called the CEO of my company and explained to him that I was going to get involved in politics. He asked what I was going to run for, and when I said, "United States Congress," he replied, "Wow. I thought you were going to say city council or something like that." I assured him that I would campaign on evenings and weekends and my work would not suffer. Thankfully, I had built up enough trust with him that he agreed to support me. Really big green light.

If any of these conversations went badly, I was committed to halt the process and not run for Congress. The final and maybe most significant conversation was with the Oversight Team of Vintage Fellowship. If our leadership team was not on board with me running, I wouldn't do it.

The ten people on our Oversight Team met on a Sunday afternoon at our church building to discuss the possibilities. With wisdom and grace, these women and men asked a lot of hard questions about my workload, my focus, and my motivation. I didn't mind the probing because I have always relied on their discernment.

Providentially, we were already in an ordination process with Vanessa. She has always been more than just a "pastor's wife." She has been my equal partner in ministry and had sensed that her calling was to be even more involved in the leadership of our church. The Oversight Team and our congregation were on the road of recognizing and affirming that calling by officially ordaining her as a pastor in our church. We have always functioned like we were driving this thing together, but with her becoming copastor of the church, we would be switching seats in the front of the car. She would take over driving and I would move to the passenger seat. The plan was for Vanessa to increase her preaching and shepherding duties so that I could spend more of my resources on the campaign. The Oversight Team loved this idea and gave us their blessing. The final green light.

The following Sunday, I stood before our congregation to tell them that I was going to run for Congress. I have made thousands of announcements in front of churches throughout my ministry, but this one felt different. I knew that some people inherently fear change and would be apprehensive about what this would mean. I didn't want anyone to feel like I was abandoning them or the church. I was sensitive to the fact that not everyone in our church votes the same way, and some might not share my thoughts about the direction of the country. Moreover, I didn't want to give the impression that I expected everyone to be on board with this new direction for me.

As I told them about my plans, I tried to be very clear. "This is not something *we* are doing," I said. "This is something *I* am doing. While I would love anyone's and even everyone's help, I want you to know that Robb 2018 is not going to be a ministry of Vintage Fellowship. In fact, some of you probably won't even vote for me, and that's okay."

I meant the words I said. My campaign for Congress wasn't mentioned again during a church service at Vintage.

Following that worship gathering, there were a lot of hugs and expressions of support. I knew that I was experiencing something special. When we had started Vintage more than a decade earlier, we often repeated that our goal was for Vintage to be the most authentic church in the world. For ten years as a fundamentalist pastor, I couldn't be myself. I couldn't say what I really thought for fear that I would be fired. We wanted to create a safe place for everyone—including the pastors—to be themselves. This group of people was giving me the freedom to pursue my passions and interests. They were letting me be me.

I wanted to carry that same value throughout the campaign. I made a personal commitment—and shared it with Vanessa for both support and accountability—that I was never going to pander for votes. I was going to tell people what I really believe. If Arkansas was ready for someone like me to represent them in Washington, great. But if not, I could be content with that, as long as I stayed true to myself.

My decision to get personally involved in politics forced us to wrestle with the questions that live at the intersection of church and state—questions about the purpose of church and government, how the Bible is interpreted, and even how political involvement by church leaders could impact their churches' tax-exempt status. These questions can be complicated, and people have very different approaches to them. I would have to be clear, in my own mind and in how I communicated, about why I think being active in government is important for the church and its leaders as well as what I was trying to accomplish through my engagement.

One of the big questions debated by Christians is "Who is responsible to help people: the church or the government?" Many Christians take a libertarian approach to this question, insisting that the purpose of government is not to provide a social safety net, and if someone should find themselves in need, the church is the place they should turn for help. Many argue in this approach that taxation is, at worst, theft, and, at best, compulsory charity.

This approach raises two critical questions. First, on a very practical level, can the church effectively meet people's needs? The average church in America has seventy people, representing approximately forty families. The average household income in America is just a hair over $56,000. Assuming each household actually tithes to their church, the average annual budget of a church would be $224,000.

Now imagine that one person in that average church has a cancer diagnosis and needs treatment that insurance does not cover. The average cost of treatment is $150,000. It is no wonder that health-care costs have become a leading cause of bankruptcy for American families. If the church is solely responsible to help people in need, health-care costs may well bankrupt churches as well.

The stark reality is that the average church in America could not meet the needs of one member with a cancer diagnosis, let alone two or more concurrently. And this is to say nothing of those in their community who do not attend a church but would still be in need. It is simply impractical to suggest that churches should provide a social safety net because it is "not the job" of the government to do so.

Maybe seeing that they cannot meet all the needs, Christians need to ask themselves a second critical question: who can and should be helped?

The ideal answer to this question is anyone in need, but it rarely works out that way. Churches have to distribute wisely what benevolence funds they have. This often leads to judgments about someone's worthiness of receiving help. Paul's admonition in 2 Thessalonians 3:10 that "Anyone unwilling to work should not eat" is often quoted in a literalist way as a mechanism to weed out the unemployed from being eligible for charity. A conservative ethos is reinforced. The church helps those who help themselves.

I'm not suggesting that churches shouldn't be judicious in how they steward the offerings of their members. Our own Oversight Team at Vintage often struggles with what kind of help to offer and how much is appropriate. I am suggesting that it is impractical, and maybe even disingenuous, to make the argument that the government doesn't play a critical role in helping people. Churches simply cannot fill in the gaps. They can't, and maybe even won't, in many cases.

I advocate for a more holistic approach. Rather than perpetuating a secular-versus-sacred divide for how people exist in the world, churches ought to teach people to live the totality of their lives—at church, at home, at work, in their neighborhoods, and in the voting booth—according to the principles of love, humility, and self-sacrifice.

Paying my taxes, for example, is a spiritual activity. When I do so, I am following the words of Jesus to give to Caesar what is Caesar's. I am being a member of a society through which I can help meet the needs of others and promote the common good. Paying my fair share in taxes is one of the many ways I love my neighbor as myself.

A second issue that emerges at the intersection of church and state is the question of what Christians are trying to accomplish by engaging in politics. Are Christians called to preserve a culture in which they feel most comfortable? Are they trying to win a culture war? Should they seek their own self-interests at the expense of others?

It is inaccurate to paint with too broad a brush how churches have chosen to resolve this tension. Some operate with a strong distinction between the secular and the sacred, seeing political involvement as a worldly endeavor that is outside of the church's mission, in which case a pastor should be the last person pursuing elected office. Others encourage individual Christians to participate according to their own conscience. There are churches, like Vintage, that believe that political involvement can and should be a part of what it means to live out the gospel. Others still, especially many who end up as spokespeople for evangelicalism in the media, advocate for the church being very involved in shaping the future of the country by preserving a conservative culture.

This final group, a significant subset of white evangelical

Christians commonly referred to as the Religious Right, typically believe that America is a "Christian nation," founded on biblical principles, and that the government should reflect these principles. They tend to be politically conservative, emphasizing social issues such as school prayer, abortion, and traditional marriage. In their worldview, secular humanists have infiltrated America's institutions with the purpose of undermining the religious foundations of our country.

People who affiliate with the Religious Right frequently adopt a persecution mind-set, in which they see themselves as a faithful remnant that is being treated unfairly because of their faith. Very often, they have seen the courts in the United States as the mechanism through which secular humanists have been able to push their agenda. For this reason, the Religious Right has trained its voters to care most deeply about the political balance of the Supreme Court, making it the singular issue on which most white evangelical Christians vote—and not strictly for overturning *Roe v. Wade*, I would argue, but for the purpose of gaining and preserving a conservative majority on the Court.

Churches that align with the Religious Right often distribute carefully crafted voter guides to their congregations. While they are unable to officially endorse a candidate for fear of losing their tax-exempt status, the voter guides are worded in such a way as to lead voters to the conclusion that one candidate supports their brand of Christian values while another candidate does not. When I started my campaign, I made the decision to ignore requests to answer surveys for these types of voters' guides. I did so because the questions frequently fail to allow for nuanced answers to questions, and giving a simplistic answer to the issue of abortion, for instance, would not accurately reflect my position. I also know how these guides are used to subtly manipulate voters. I did not want to be a party to that.

Refusing to respond to these surveys may not have been the best decision I made in the campaign. One voter guide distributed in churches in my district stated that I chose not to answer their questions and published my cell phone number. On multiple occasions, I received calls from voters asking why I didn't participate in the guide and asking if I was going to support "biblical values." These calls turned into lengthy conversations with well-meaning folks. I don't think I convinced any of them to vote for me, but I told all of them how happy I was that they were engaged voters.

The most memorable call came from a man in a small town several hours from my hometown. I let the call go to voice mail and later listened to his four-minute-long message about how terrible it was that I refused to take a stand on "biblical values" by answering the survey questions. From his tone, I decided it wasn't worth the effort to call him back. A few days later, I was knocking on doors in his town. Without realizing it, I was at his house. After I introduced myself, he said, "I left you a voice mail. I'm so glad you stopped by to talk to me." We chatted politely for about twenty minutes. When I was finally able to extradite myself from the conversation, I walked past the Trump sign in his yard, knowing that he was not going to cast his vote for me.

It is a tremendously difficult proposition to win the votes of people who have been indoctrinated by the Religious Right to vote differently, but I have not given up hope because shifts in the voting pattern of Christians have happened. Historically, white evangelicals in America have not always been a monolith of conservative voters. In the 1960s, many evangelical pastors and leaders, including Billy Graham, were supportive of reproductive rights. *Newsweek* declared 1976 the "year of the evangelicals" and wrote a glowing story about how religious voters would propel Jimmy Carter to the presidency. Even today, a growing number of progressive evangelicals are working to provide a counterbalance to the Religious Right's influence.

In the course of my campaign, I did three different "Ask Me Anything" forums on Reddit. Without fail, I was asked about my views on the separation of church and state. I could tell each time by how the questions were phrased that the questioner feared I was a member of the Religious Right who was trying to impose my religion on others. I assured them that while my faith compelled me to become personally involved, I was not trying to "take America back for Jesus." I was committed to fighting for the equal protection of all people, no matter how they believe or if they believe at all. For me, faith is the motivation to build a more just and generous society in which everyone has the same liberty and opportunity.

My inclination is driven by two historical examples of pastors who dared to go to the intersection of church and state and make their voices heard.

The first was Roger Williams, an early settler in the American colonies. He came to the colonies because of his discomfort with the influence the British government had over the Church of England. As a Puritan pastor, he lived and ministered in Massachusetts. However, he resisted other Puritan leaders whom he thought were perpetuating the mistakes of their homeland by mistreating Native people and insisting that all colonists in Massachusetts belong to Puritan churches.

Ultimately, Roger Williams was condemned as a heretic and exiled from Massachusetts. He ended up founding Rhode Island as the first American colony to protect religious freedom. Williams's teachings about the separation of church and state profoundly influenced the framers of the U.S. Constitution. Williams demonstrates to me that a pastor can engage in the public square on principle, resist the prevailing ecclesiastical mood, and help to shape the future of a society. As a pastor and leader whose own faith was driving his involvement in government, Williams used his influence to protect and advocate for those who believed differently than he did. I think America could use a new generation of pastors like Roger Williams.

I also drew inspiration from German pastor Dietrich Bonhoeffer. Bonhoeffer grew up with profound privilege. He was able to receive an education and write with relative comfort, but with the rise of Nazism, that comfort came to an end. His legacy has been lionized and even bastardized in recent years by evangelical biographers trying to claim him as their own. But for me, Bonhoeffer serves as an example of a Christian who finally recognized that he could not sit on the sidelines of crisis in his church and country any longer. After spending years in the United States and elsewhere, he returned to Germany in 1939 to help train young pastors in a seminary for those who resisted the German church's capitulation to Adolf Hitler. His own resistance to Hitler became so intense that he ended up participating in a plot to assassinate the German leader. He was arrested for his activities and ultimately died in a concentration camp.

As I was launching my campaign, I told friends that I felt like I was having my own "Bonhoeffer moment." While I certainly wasn't suggesting going to the extreme he did, I knew that I could no longer be silent about the direction of our country. My faith was compelling me to become involved in ways I never would have imagined. Roger Williams and Dietrich Bonhoeffer tried to do what they could to meet the challenges of their times. I would do the same as a candidate for the U.S. Congress from Arkansas's Third District.

4

Never Read the Comments Section

★ ★ ★

Vitriol, Social Media,
and Suspending Judgment

I had thought that all of the necessary precampaign conversations had taken place, but I was mistaken. Just before I launched my campaign, I got a call from Sam, one of the Brand New Congress folks who had coached me on being a candidate. Sam is one of the most exuberant people I've ever met. His passion is infectious. But on this call, he was serious.

"Robb, you're about to be in the public eye like never before," he said. "It's time I ask you *the* question." I gulped as he continued. "Is there anything you need to tell me? If there is, it's better that we discuss it now. If there are skeletons in your closet, they will come out."

Nothing really prepares you for that kind of question. I took a deep breath.

I told Sam about how we lost our home during the housing crisis of 2008. When we moved to Arkansas to start Vintage Fellowship, we were unable to sell our home in Michigan. After years of trying and some unfortunate renters, we had no option but to give it back to the bank in a deed in lieu of foreclosure. For years, I carried a lot of shame about losing our house. I felt like I had let Vanessa and my family down. Sam listened and then gently replied, "Robb, you're a regular person. These things happen to regular people. If nothing else, it'll make you more relatable if it comes up."

I sighed and continued, "Sam, I've got some family members whose stories are their own, and I really don't want them to be forced to tell them. One is bisexual. Another has been struggling with mental illness and has even been suicidal lately." Again, Sam assured me that he didn't think members of my family would have their personal stories made public, but if they did, it would reflect poorly on whoever did it, not my family members.

"Anything else?" Sam asked.

"Well, I got a speeding ticket a couple of weeks ago," I said sheepishly.

"I think we're going to be okay," Sam said. "Let's do this thing." And so we did.

My campaign officially launched on May 23, 2017. It was 364 days before my name would appear on the Republican primary ballot. I wasn't alone launching then. Four other Brand New Congress (BNC) candidates started campaigning that same day. We did a live stream together, thinking that our coordinated effort would lead to greater visibility. We were joined by two other BNC candidates who had previously announced their campaigns: Cori Bush from Missouri and Paula Jean Swearengin from West Virginia.

Our live stream included a couple of other Congress Camp alumni, Alexandria Ocasio-Cortez and Michael Hepburn. Also announcing were Adrienne Bell from Houston and Anthony Clark from Chicago. Adrienne and Anthony were teachers, hoping to expand their influence from the classroom to the halls of Congress. It was a fun evening in which we discussed our shared vision for the country. We proposed bold ideas to solve the problems associated with our health-care system and our criminal justice system. We talked about jobs and the economy, the environment and education.

When our live stream ended, I knew that several thousand people around the country had tuned in. Thousands more would see it on social media. What we were trying to do as Brand New Congress candidates, working together across parties and districts, had never been done. I hoped our influence would grow.

Regardless, now the campaign had begun. The paperwork was filed. My website and social media were up and running. The announcement was made. I was a candidate for the U.S. House of Representatives.

I woke up the next morning to a buzzing cell phone. It didn't stop buzzing all day.

Interspersed with the texts and messages from family and friends congratulating me on my campaign launch were several media requests. I drove to local television studios to do sit-down interviews. I talked to newspaper reporters on the phone from my car. I booked radio and podcast interviews. Local and national media were both interested in hearing the story of a Christian pastor running a grassroots long-shot campaign for Congress as a progressive Republican in highly conservative Arkansas.

I heard author and speaker Rob Bell say one time that when he's doing media interviews to promote a book he's written, he's asked the same seven questions each time. I discovered that this is also true when you're running for office. Everyone I talked to wanted me to discuss the same things. They wanted to know about my church. They wanted to know if I had voted for President Trump or for Hillary Clinton. They wanted to know why I was running as a Republican if I had progressive views on the issues. They wanted to know my stand on abortion.

Throughout all of those interviews, I learned that I am very good at message discipline. Some politicians can't help but meander when they answer questions, often unintentionally raising even more questions. When I find an answer with which I'm satisfied, I am able to repeat it consistently. For some reason, I don't get bored with the answer. I knew this would serve me well throughout the campaign.

The most high-profile interview request came from a producer with Fox News. A British commentator named Steve

Hilton was starting a new show on Fox News called *The Next Revolution*. He was scheduled to have Zack Exley, Brand New Congress's founder in the studio, and wanted to do a segment about me, shot in our home.

We only had a day or two to get ready. For years Vanessa has repeated the phrase "nothing cleans like company" when we are getting our house straightened up to host friends or family. That saying has never been truer than when a camera crew from a major cable news outlet is coming to your home. She even cleaned the baseboards, as if they were going to appear on national television.

When the crew arrived, we sat in my dining room and discussed the same basic questions everyone else had asked me. I was prepared, stayed on message, and thought that portion went well. The rest of it felt surreal. They wanted b-roll footage of my campaign, so I convinced a few friends to don their purple "Robb 2018" T-shirts and pretend to canvass my neighborhood while the cameras rolled. They also wanted a shot of Vanessa and me relaxing in our living room, so they positioned us awkwardly on a couch. I don't think we had ever sat that way on that couch—a good reminder that not everything you see on the news is real.

A couple of days later, when the segment aired, one of our friends threw a watch party. This was really helpful for Vanessa and me because we don't have cable and wouldn't be able to watch the segment live. About twenty friends and supporters gathered in our friend's living room. I had never seen myself on national television. We watched and cheered.

Before the segment had even ended, my phone buzzed again. Someone I had never met posted a Facebook message to my campaign page. It simply read, "Communist." A few minutes later, a second message arrived. It called me a socialist pig. The excitement and elation of the moment were lost to a couple of Internet trolls.

People often joke that you should never read the comments section of an article or news story. Comments sections are

people make, the positions they hold, and the issues for which they advocate are all informed by their life experiences. Understanding those choices, positions, and issues is easier if you know those people's stories. Rather than making assumptions from our own perspectives, suspended judgment forces us to examine things from the vantage point of the other, which takes time and work.

One of my college professors required students to use primary sources for research papers. Instead of relying on what others had said or written about a historical figure, we had to take the time to find out what that person had actually said. It was laborious and frustrating at times, but it compelled us to develop a deeper and more authentic understanding of whomever we were researching. The time and effort are worth it. In fact, because we are in the Information Age, equipped with ubiquitous devices connected to the Internet, finding primary sources, especially from our political leaders, has never been easier. Candidates for office have websites, social media accounts, speeches on YouTube, and position papers available. These sources let candidates speak for themselves without the filter of a political pundit's interpretation.

Taking this another important step, Brené Brown says, "Empathy is not connecting to an experience, it's connecting to the emotions that underpin an experience."[2] While we may not be able to grasp the circumstances that others have experienced, we do share the underlying fears, anger, and shame that are part of our common humanity. By tapping into these emotions, we can come to see that others are driven to their conclusions in an understandable way.

In the course of my campaign, I had conversations with thousands of voters. A few of those exchanges stand out for me. I met a woman who told me about her elderly father, who was unable to retire because he and his diabetic wife could not afford insulin for her if they lost his employer-provided health insurance. I met a young professional who was riddled with anxiety because of his student loan debt. I met a black mother who asked me if the lives of her sons mattered. I met teenagers who were organizing rallies in the wake of another tragic school shooting.

Their stories moved me. Their emotions touched me. They raised questions I could not shake.

Wouldn't it make sense for a family struggling to pay their medical bills to be passionate about making sure every other family in America has adequate health coverage so that they don't have to go through similar hardship? Who has not wondered how they're going to make ends meet?

Wouldn't it make sense for a young person to question an economic system in which they feel left behind? Who has not lost sleep over how a personal financial crisis is going to be resolved?

Wouldn't it make sense for a person of color to distrust authority figures who may profile their teenage children who are driving home at night? Who has not feared that our kids won't make it home safely?

Wouldn't it make sense for high schoolers to be traumatized by the epidemic of gun violence that has been omnipresent through their formative years? Who has not felt powerless at times?

More than anything, I wanted to go to Washington and be the voice for all such people, their representative in Congress.

Empathy for another—truly understanding one another's fear, anger, and shame—is the path to suspended judgment. And suspended judgment is what we need to ensure that our culture is not divided by hurtful words spoken or posted in haste to score cheap political points.

Jesus told us in John 7:24 to "judge with right judgment." Rarely does that happen when we make snap judgments—and even more rarely do we find right judgments in the comments section.

5

No, Really, I Am a Republican

★ ★ ★

Partisan Stereotypes
and Evolving Orthodoxy

The most common questions I answered throughout the campaign were about my affiliation with the Republican Party. They took different forms, but the essence of the questions was the same: "If you're a progressive, why run as a Republican?" "Why not run as a Democrat?" "You're not really a Republican, are you?"

People tend to think in stereotypes. They see what they have been conditioned to see. When something comes along that challenges their preconceived ideas, they either try to redefine it or they reject it. They try to put it into a familiar category or they think it's an anomaly. Voters in this day and age simply aren't used to a Republican who espouses progressive views. They didn't quite know what to make of me. I joked that I was a unicorn. I think that every reporter I talked to during the campaign asked me about this. So did people at every house party or voter forum. I was plagued with these questions on social media.

Almost daily during the campaign, I had to insist that I was a real thing, an actual Republican who was questioning current party orthodoxy and resisting the party establishment. I am quite confident that voters and reporters alike were skeptical of how I answered these questions, but I always told the truth.

First I would explain that my congressional district is a bright-red district. My opponent, Representative Steve Womack, had not faced a primary challenger since he was first elected. The Democratic Party hadn't even fielded a candidate in the past two elections. Womack had never received less than 72 percent of the vote. In November 2018 Arkansas's Third Congressional District was going to send a Republican to Washington.

Therefore, the best chance anyone had to beat Congressman Womack was in the Republican primary in May 2018, rather than in the general election. If a well-organized grassroots campaign energized enough voters, it could pull off a surprise upset in a low-voter-turnout primary election. I thought that we could connect with three types of voters: younger evangelicals who grew up Republican but were disaffected by current GOP leadership, antiestablishment voters who overwhelmingly supported President Trump in Arkansas but may be interested in "draining the swamp" of a career politician like Congressman Womack, and Democrats and Independents who would be willing to vote in the Republican primary since Arkansas has open primaries.

I spoke to several progressive groups, including local Indivisible chapters that were filled with typically Democratic voters. I would tell them that my goal was simply to be their favorite Republican. If they would be willing to do the same thing I was doing—putting the needs of people ahead of party loyalty—then together we could shock everyone. If there weren't competitive primaries on the Democratic ticket in my district and if I could reach enough voters, I figured we might have a chance.

I also made clear, however, that I was not a charlatan who changed parties on some kind of political calculation. I am a born-and-bred Republican. I ran as a Republican because I *am* a Republican. Far from being some kind of RINO (Republican in Name Only), I share the deeply ingrained Republican values of liberty from the tyranny of the government, optimism about each person's opportunity in America, and responsibility and accountability. I have been deeply bothered when I've seen my party move away from these values at times, but that didn't change my personal affinity to the principles themselves.

I wanted to be my authentic self. My authentic self is not a Democrat. My authentic self is a Republican who used to be very conservative but has grown very progressive in the last decade. I'm a Republican who recognizes the historical values of my party and thinks it's been hijacked by people who don't share those values. I am a Republican who is profoundly troubled by my party's nomination and ultimate election of Donald Trump.

As a dissatisfied Republican, the question I had to ask myself is whether I should leave my party or stay in it and try to fight for its future. I decided to be an agent of change within the GOP rather than abandon it. Throughout their history, political parties have changed and evolved. They are not static, monolithic blocs. Political parties have proven to be malleable and movable organizations. Change is not just possible; it regularly happens within America's political parties.

The last forty years of Republican policy have been dominated by conservative thinking, but the Grand Old Party used to be the progressive party in American politics. In fact, the Republican Party platform of 1956 called for equal pay for women, increasing the minimum wage, strengthening labor unions, and expanding programs like Social Security. These positions are far from Republican orthodoxy today, but they used to be. If the GOP once embraced and advocated for progressive policy, why couldn't it do so again?

Many of the issues I care about have the historical precedent of being championed by prominent Republicans. The last significant immigration reform, including granting amnesty to undocumented people, was signed into law by President Ronald Reagan, the Republican icon. The Environmental Protection Agency was created by a Republican president, Richard Nixon, because he recognized that caring for the planet should not be a partisan issue. It was a Republican president, Dwight Eisenhower, who coined the critical phrase "military industrial complex," made sure the wealthiest Americans paid their fair share in taxes, and spent massive federal dollars on infrastructure and the interstate highway system.

I learned that some members of the Arkansas Republican establishment nicknamed me the "Bernie Sanders Republican." As much as I liked this moniker, given the fact that Senator Sanders consistently polls as the most popular politician in the country, I figured it wasn't the branding that would best serve me. I started to refer to myself as an "Eisenhower Republican," because I wanted people to recognize that I was not trying to do something that had never been done. I was trying to stand on the shoulders of other Republican leaders who fought for progressive ideas.

And I wasn't alone. In the course of my campaign, I came to know other Republicans who were running for Congress around the country on progressive and moderate platforms. On a couple of occasions, I convened conference calls with Republican congressional candidates in New Jersey, Ohio, Georgia, Tennessee, North Carolina, and California. All of us were opposed to the president's agenda and were motivated to run because we wanted to be part of a political party that was not dominated by conservative dogma. Time will tell if we were waging hopeless campaigns or if we were on the cutting edge of a new movement. I'm willing to wait and see what fruit our efforts produce.

Any serious recalibration of Republican policy positions needs to address four of the most divisive issues: abortion, health care, immigration, and climate change. I didn't shy away from these controversial subjects but talked often of them during my campaign as a way of differentiating myself from the Republicans people typically see on television. I shared how my own thinking on these issues evolved. I tried to connect my positions to historic Republican values. I asked voters to think of these issues from a fresh moral and economic perspective. If the Republican Party is going to remain relevant, I believe it must do the same.

Abortion

Since the ascendancy of the Religious Right in Republican politics, the single most important issue to conservative Christian voters has been abortion. Growing up in a fundamentalist home, I was ardently pro-life. I attended the March for Life in Washington as a teenager and had always felt strongly that protecting life in the womb was of fundamental importance. Vanessa and I became foster parents and ultimately adopted one of our children, because I had long believed that pro-lifers need to put their convictions into action, not just votes.

However, as my theological and political beliefs evolved, I began to think differently about abortion. While I remained personally pro-life, I was no longer a single-issue voter. I came to see being pro-life as a more holistic position. Life outside the womb needs to be as valued as life in the womb. Making sure all people have health care, educational opportunities, and the possibility of living their lives with freedom all became expressions of my pro-life stance.

Further, I began to question the tactics used by the pro-life movement in America. For pro-life voters, overturning *Roe v. Wade* by getting pro-life justices on the Supreme Court has become the key to achieving their goals. Yet I began to wonder if pro-life activists actually care more about preserving the issue as a fund-raising and voter turnout tool than they care about reducing the number of abortions. It seems to me that if you are pro-life, your goal ought to be seeing the fewest number of abortions possible.

I began to research what actually reduces abortion rates in America, and what I found surprised me. In states where access to abortion services is limited, abortion rates actually go up. Often these limitations are coupled with decreases in sex education, access to health care, and contraception. When enacted with such an ideologically driven agenda, criminalizing abortions is not the way to reduce them.

On the other hand, when women have greater access to health care, abortion rates go down. Contrary to the fear-mongering associated with much of the pro-life movement, abortion rates in 2016 were actually lower than they were in 1973 when abortion was legalized. When the government invests in education in general, and sex education in particular—including providing access to contraception—abortion rates go down. When tangible steps are taken to reduce poverty, abortion rates go down. Therefore, as a pro-life person, I believe the best path to decreasing abortions in America is to expand health care, education, and the social safety net.

I feared that making this argument would fail to satisfy anyone. On the campaign trail, I found that, while they were pleased that I wouldn't vote to criminalize or outlaw abortion, pro-choice voters didn't like that I still called myself pro-life. Pro-life voters were also displeased because I wouldn't commit to overturning *Roe v. Wade*. I was caught in a double bind. I decided that I would honor the commitment I made to not troll for votes while campaigning. I would tell people what I actually believe would be best for the country and let the chips fall where they may.

Health Care

From 2012 on, Republican congressional candidates across the country campaigned on a commitment to repeal and replace the Affordable Care Act, commonly called Obamacare. I believed that their motivation was far more partisan and obstructionist than it was to make sure that the most Americans possible have health coverage. I think these Republican leaders put denying President Obama his signature legislative achievement ahead of the needs of people.

This kind of blatant partisanship didn't sit well with me. I believe that in one of the wealthiest countries in the world, it is morally unacceptable that people don't have adequate access to health care. As a Christian, I looked to the example of Jesus, who consistently took responsibility for the health of others and rejected the argument that individuals are only responsible for themselves. We are all responsible for one another. Nobody should suffer or die because they can't afford insurance. Families shouldn't be bankrupted by medical bills. People shouldn't have to suffer the indignity of begging for help on crowdfunding websites just to get the care they need.

Advocating for Medicare for All was a central theme of my campaign. I had to take this position for moral reasons. But it's also a position that makes good economic sense.

The health-care system as presently constituted in America is an undue burden on small business owners. Since current regulations require small business owners to provide health coverage for their employees, health care is actually an issue with profound implications for job growth and economic expansion. A small business owner in my district explained to me that if he was free of this regulation, he would be able to grow his business without hesitation. I told his story frequently on the campaign trail.

I also invited voters to imagine a woman working for a big corporation in our district. Each and every day she was sitting at her desk, doing a job she wasn't passionate about, even though she may have the idea for a new company that could be the next great American success story. But she simply couldn't afford to quit her job and chase her dreams because she had a daughter at home with a preexisting condition. She can't lose her health coverage. Medicare for All would actually free up the next generation of entrepreneurs to start new businesses.

I thought an argument could be made to Republican voters that a system like Medicare for All would actually be in keeping with the Republican values of limited government overreach into the lives of citizens and expanding economic opportunity.

When I started my campaign, I think I was the only Republican running for office making the case for Medicare for All. By the spring of 2018, the latest polling showed that 37 percent of Republicans supported Medicare for All. By the end of 2018, those numbers had risen to 54 percent of Republicans. A majority of Republican voters—not their elected leaders yet, but voters—support universal health care. I've joked with friends that I take personal credit for this, but the reality is that an increasing number of people across the political spectrum recognize the moral and economic benefits of Medicare for All—and that is a very good thing.

Immigration

Throughout the 2018 campaign, President Trump's insistence on building a wall along the southern U.S. border kept the issue of immigration in the headlines, but the saga of Victor Galindo brought the matter home to my district. Victor was originally from Mexico but had been living in the United States for over two decades. In the process of trying to renew his visa, Victor found out that some of his paperwork was wrong, and he was actually undocumented. As soon as Immigration and Customs Enforcement (ICE) was notified, Victor was alerted that he was going to be deported, leaving behind his wife and four children—all because of a clerical error.

Victor's church rallied, asking people to sign a petition of support for him. Congressman Steve Womack refused to intervene on Victor's behalf, but I decided that his story needed to be told. I used as much of my platform as I could to advocate for Victor because his story is tragically common. Victor's experience is indicative of so many others. He was the victim of a complicated and heartless process where mercy and understanding are trumped by strict adherence to an arbitrary code set forth in our immigration laws.

Over the years, people's ability to enter the country with documentation has become so tremendously burdensome that, stunningly, risking life and limb to enter the country without documentation is the easier option. Just like water finds the path of least resistance as it flows, so too do people who are migrating. Republicans, who consistently rail against a bloated governmental bureaucracy that oppresses regular people, should see comprehensive immigration reform that includes a swift path to citizenship as an issue to support. Instead of advocating for the elimination of the Department of Education, Republicans ought to call for ICE to be abolished because, since its founding in 2003, it has proven to be more harmful to families than any other government agency.

Before the election of Donald Trump, it was not uncommon for Republican leaders to call for needed immigration reform. More than once during my campaign, I shared a YouTube video of a 1980 Republican presidential debate in which both candidates, Ronald Reagan and George Bush, rejected the politics of fear and called for people to be welcomed into our country. Maybe more than anything else, I've been inspired by the words of President Reagan when he spoke of the United States being a shining city on a hill, a welcoming and hopeful place where people from all over the world could find opportunity.

Sadly, Victor was deported not long after the May 2018 primary. I believe that unless the Republican Party rejects the unorthodoxy of Trumpism and returns to its historic value of welcoming immigrants and refugees, it risks permanently becoming a minority party in America.

Climate Change

For the past several decades, the Republican Party has completely abandoned environmental issues to the Democratic Party, which is inexplicable to me. Addressing climate change would give Republicans an opportunity to highlight their long commitment to economic growth and job creation through innovation. When they frame the debate as a choice between taking care of the environment or growing the economy, they not only give voters a false dichotomy, they also retreat from their position as the party of optimistic prosperity.

But my commitment to environmental issues is far more than a pragmatic and economic one. It's a matter of faith for me. I can't read past the first few pages of my Bible without being struck with how the opening story in my faith tradition is one in which creation is seen as the work of the divine. God wanted people to enjoy and steward the world, not pollute and consume it. Supporting policies that address climate change, in my mind, is completely consistent with biblical teaching. Given the Bible's rather plain injunctions that humanity has the responsibility to care for the planet, it is strange to me that so many reliably Republican voters in the Religious Right have rejected addressing climate change. I have come to realize that their resistance is a theological one rooted in eschatology, the doctrine of the end of the world.

Many evangelicals believe in an end-times scenario popularized by the *Left Behind* books in which the church is Raptured out of the world, followed by a tribulation period in which things become increasingly worse, before Jesus finally returns to Earth to set up his millennial kingdom. For these Christians, this is the only way human history can end. They reason that if you believe the Bible, you cannot believe the scientists who say human history could end in any other manner.

Since this divide has become deeply entrenched, my hope for the future lies in young evangelicals who recognize both the danger posed by climate change and the biblical call to care for the environment. I believe the next generation will respond well to leaders in either party who will boldly make the case for climate change action on moral and economic grounds.

The Republican Party was born out of the antislavery movement of the 1850s. It was led to prominence by Abraham Lincoln. For more than a hundred years, the Republican Party stood for equal opportunity for all people. In recent decades, the Grand Old Party has become more known for who and what it is against rather than who and what it is for, and has moved away from its historic values. By rejecting progressive ideas and embracing conservative ones, the party has morphed into a home for people motivated by their fear of change. I don't know what the future of the Republican Party will be. If the Trump presidency ends up decimating the Republican Party, as many prognosticators claim, my hope is that from its ashes will emerge a grand new party that is animated by the progressive values that once made it so vital.

6

The Myth of Objectivity

★ ★ ★

Bias, Echo Chambers,
and Life under the Camera

During the course of my campaign, I had thousands of conversations with people across Arkansas's Third District. I had hundreds of interactions online. I did scores of media interviews. In the midst of all of these exchanges, three specific, rather surreal ones stand out, each illustrating important lessons I learned firsthand as a candidate.

The first happened at a Starbucks. I was headed in to get a coffee and do some work on my laptop when I noticed a particular customer sitting near the door. It was Congressman Steve Womack. We didn't make eye contact as I went in, but after I ordered, I sat where I could see him. I immediately pulled out my computer and jumped on a messaging app to let some friends know that he and I were in the same place at the same time. My phone was getting its screen replaced at the time, so I couldn't snap a picture. I was sad not to be able to document a face-to-face encounter with my opponent in the wild.

I was determined to talk to him. When he stood up to leave, I gathered my stuff and hurried to catch up with him in the parking lot.

"Congressman Womack," I called, reaching out my hand to shake his. "I'm Robb Ryerse."

"Hello, Robb. Nice to meet you. How do you pronounce your last name again?" he replied.

He knows who I am, I thought.

We chatted briefly about the president, and then I made a suggestion: "You know, we ought to have some voter forums together in the spring when the primary gets closer."

He was not interested. "Well, in the spring, I'll be working on marking up appropriations bills," he said.

"That's assuming you guys actually pass a budget," I said. I couldn't believe I resorted to sarcasm.

Congressman Womack didn't laugh. And he never did a voter forum with me.

After we parted, I headed back into Starbucks to report to my friends what had happened. They all laughed about our interaction and encouraged me. But the more I thought about it, I came to an important realization: our elected leaders are not celebrities. They are not a special class of people who got their positions because of some elevated intellect or ability. They are regular people who drink coffee at Starbucks.

My district is home to one of the world's most amazing art museums, the Crystal Bridges Museum of American Art. Our family often wanders around Crystal Bridges to both relax and be inspired. More than once, I've stood before a painting, usually something in the modern wing, and heard other people talking about how they could have done the very thing that is hanging on the wall. It looks so easy; anybody could do it. I'm always tempted to yell, "But the artist actually did it!"

The same is true with politics. The reason many of our leaders are in office is not because they are better, smarter, or more skilled than the rest of us. The reason they are in office is because they ran for it. They actually did it.

When I left Starbucks that day, I began to think of myself as Congressman Womack's equal.

Another interaction that I'll never forget happened when my phone rang one evening. I was sitting on my back porch, unwinding from a busy day of campaigning with a cigar and a beer. The incoming call was from a number I didn't recognize, but it was from the city of Ithaca, New York, which wasn't terribly far from where I lived when I was in high school, so I decided to answer it.

"This is Robb. May I help you?" I said like I do whenever I answer the phone from an unknown number.

"Are you running for Congress?" the voice on the other end of the line said quickly.

"Yes, I am. Are you with a media organization?" I replied.

"No, but I've got some questions for you," he said.

"Okay," I said, feeling kind of leery.

He went on to ask what I thought my chances of winning were and what I planned to do if I lost. These were unusual questions, and I was taken aback. I gathered myself and explained that I was focused on campaigning, that my candidacy was a long shot, but all of my focus was on the May 22 primary, and that I hadn't thought about May 23 yet.

He seemed undeterred. I could tell he had something specific in mind that he wanted to tell me, but I had no idea what it was. Then he came out with it. "Well, when you lose, I think you should run for Speaker of the House."

Wait, what? I thought. *This is the worst backhanded compliment I've ever received.*

He explained that the Speaker of the House doesn't have to actually be a member of the House of Representatives, and he was thinking that I was the right kind of person to challenge then-Speaker Paul Ryan. He was convinced that if I started campaigning for it, I could convince the necessary 218 representatives to vote for me.

"Well, that's an interesting idea. Thanks for calling," was all I could muster.

When I finally got off the phone with him, I called Scott, my campaign manager, and told him to begin preparing for the second stage of my campaign. Right after I couldn't even win my own district, I would begin a campaign for the third-most powerful position in the whole country, to be chosen by people who had actually won their races. Scott and I laughed at the absurdity of it. Then he suggested I let unknown numbers just go to voice mail.

When I returned to my cigar and beer, I thought back to my days in Bible college, learning about principles for interpreting the Bible. I remembered my professor saying to us, "If you are the first person in the history of the church to interpret a passage from the Bible in some unique way, chances are that you're wrong." He was imploring us to be humble when we read the Bible and to recognize the wisdom of those who have gone before us.

By personality, I'm drawn to the minority reports that question conventional wisdom, but I also appreciate the foolishness in thinking that I can come up with an idea no one has ever considered. Maybe this man who called me and urged me to run for Speaker of the House had one such novel idea. While he was technically correct, his idea was devoid of any practicality. We overcomplicate things to our own peril. For better or for worse, sometimes we have to work within the system as it is commonly accepted to bring about the change we desire.

On a Monday morning in mid-June 2017, I received an e-mail from an associate producer with a documentary company telling me that they wanted to chat with me about my campaign. A pleasant woman named Nicole and I talked on the phone later that day. She explained that the company she worked for, Sarah Colt Productions in New York City, was looking for a candidate to feature in a documentary they were making about how people were responding to the Trump presidency. They had read a news report about me and thought the story of a Christian pastor running as a progressive Republican would be compelling.

We talked several times before Nicole and her boss, Josh Gleason, along with a cameraman and sound technician, traveled to Arkansas. Vanessa, Scott (who is also a documentarian), and I met with them in my living room. They explained how they'd like to follow my campaign around, filming the key moments as well as the mundane realities of running for office. They wanted to capture what it's like for a regular person to mount a first-time political campaign, and after talking to several candidates around the country, my story was the one they wanted to tell.

They wanted me to grant them exclusive access to my campaign, which proved to be a sticking point. I had already met Rachel Lears, who had started making a documentary about Brand New Congress candidates. I liked Rachel a lot and wanted to participate in her documentary, but Sarah Colt Productions was asking for exclusivity. A few months later, a third company would call, asking to film my campaign for a television show they were producing.

It's surreal to have to decide if you want to open your life to a film crew, and it's even more surreal to have to choose between several. I ultimately decided to grant Josh and Nicole's request for exclusivity for no better reason than they were the ones sitting in my living room asking for it. I came to trust them and really enjoy their company, and I don't have any regrets, even though Rachel's film *Knock Down the House* ended up premiering at the Sundance Film Festival and being picked up by Netflix for national distribution. She found her story and told it movingly, focusing on my Brand New Congress sisters Alexandria Ocasio-Cortez, Paula Jean Swearengin, Cori Bush, and Amy Vilela.

Even more surreal than choosing a film crew is actually being filmed by them. On one visit to Arkansas, they were going to film a worship gathering at Vintage Fellowship. The day before, they wanted to record my sermon preparation. "You want to film me sitting at my computer?" I asked.

"Well, is that what you do?" Josh asked.

"Yeah, that's about it," I said honestly.

He probed further. "Do you think maybe you could practice your sermon out loud or something?"

"No. I haven't really done that in about two decades," I replied.

They didn't end up using the footage of me sermon-prepping. Nor did they use the hour or so of Vanessa and I comparing our calendars and making sure we had all of our son

Calvin's band rehearsals synced up. They really were getting the most mundane stuff.

One of the most memorable times of filming came after I had had a long day traveling to Little Rock and back. It was late in the evening, and Vanessa and I were debriefing our day, sitting on our bed, eating burgers we had delivered. When we finished and the crew was packing up, we learned that our cameraman, Tom, was flying from Arkansas to Los Angeles the next morning. He was going to the Academy Awards because a documentary he had shot was nominated for an Oscar.

"What is this weird life we are living?" Vanessa asked me when the house was finally quiet.

I learned pretty quickly that having a film crew capturing your every move changes the moves you make. They would film me driving in my car to a campaign stop, then jump out of the car and have me drive around the block and park again so that they could get footage without the cameraman in the car.

They positioned me for shots. They went ahead of me when I was knocking on doors to secure permission from homeowners to film on their property. They suggested activities and reactions they thought would be good for the film. Their presence was always a positive experience, but I was always conscious of it. They proved the observer effect, that the act of observing an object necessarily changes the movement of an object.

The presence of a film crew documenting my campaign proved something to me that I had always suspected: true objectivity is a myth.

Filmmakers are not objective because they have a narrative they are trying to tell. A pastor preparing a sermon is not objective when she interprets a passage of Scripture because she is always wearing the lenses of her own experience. A scientist is not objective because his laboratory tests are being funded by some bigger corporation. News reporters are not objective because they cannot escape their own perspectives on a story.

People certainly try to be fair in how they present things, but completely setting aside one's own biases is impossible.

The things that get noticed, the aspects of the story that are deemed important, and the vantage points taken are all shaped by the presuppositions, attitudes, and worldview of the one telling the story. To one extent or another, every story is staged in some way, open to interpretation, and only one aspect of a bigger narrative.

Unfortunately, many Americans fail to see the lack of objectivity in the stories they are told. I suspect that most of us can point out examples of media bias, but we tend to think that our favorite media outlets are not biased. I believe that all of us need to remember the myth of objectivity whenever we consume stories, especially those told by the now-ubiquitous twenty-four-hour news cycle.

Gone are the days when you would read a newspaper in the morning and catch the evening news on television at the end of the day. From our social media feeds to twenty-four-hour cable stations to the news sites we have bookmarked, we have unending access to what is happening around the world. Our phones notify us when breaking news is happening. A person can consume media literally nonstop, and we've never had more options. We don't have to choose between just three broadcast networks or two local newspapers. Hundreds of news sources are available, each with its own brand and seeking to carve out its own piece of the market. As such, news sources develop reputations. Consumers know that when they watch Fox News, stories are presented with a conservative slant. If you click on a HuffPost article, you will likely receive a more liberal perspective. The lack of objectivity has never been more apparent for those willing to recognize it.

Inherent subjectivity is not the same as "fake news," President Trump's popular Twitter refrain. He uses this phrase to call into question any reporting that casts him in a negative light. He wants his base to completely distrust any media with which he might disagree.

During the Republican primaries of 2016, the Trump campaign held an event at the airport in my area. Calvin and I decided to go see what all the fuss was about. We stood with a thousand or so other people and listened to then-candidate Trump talk about his vision for the country. I was appalled to hear him say that he thinks the subjects of news stories should be able to sue reporters. Such a stance undermines the First Amendment and the free press, which have always been part of the bedrock of our democracy. I was even more appalled to hear his supporters cheer.

The U.S. media must remain free to report the stories they deem newsworthy. The media have the responsibility of being a check and balance on people in power. However, I am convinced that the American people are also responsible for holding the media accountable for their product.

The solution to the myth of objectivity is not government interference with the media or any kind of regulation of the press through a coerced fairness doctrine. If Matt Drudge wants to curate headlines to coincide with his political persuasion, so be it. If the *Washington Post* decides to allocate significant resources researching one particular story while not doing the same for another story, that is their prerogative. We can address the lack of objectivity by maintaining a healthy, balanced media diet. Just like it would be unhealthy for a person to only eat fast food, so too is it unhealthy for a person to watch only one news outlet or read one website.

The danger of an unbalanced media diet is falling into or even creating an echo chamber, when the only beliefs or opinions you are exposed to reinforce your existing perspective. In today's environment, consuming media from only one perspective is all too easy. A woman could read progressive news websites in the morning, see stories shared on social media from her progressive friends throughout the day, listen to a progressive podcast during her time at the gym, and watch Rachel Maddow on MSNBC in the evening. Day after day, she could exclusively receive her news from only one perspective, completely closed off from any stories or ideas that might present information that she had not considered.

When we live in an echo chamber, confirmation bias sets in.

Confirmation bias is when we only pay attention to statistics and stories that support our existing beliefs and ideas. Alternative perspectives or challenging facts are conveniently ignored. Confirmation bias rewards a lack of curiosity by reinforcing what we already think we know, stunting our ability to grow and develop into more holistic and empathetic human beings.

Confirmation bias is a symptom of our privilege. As a white, straight, Christian man, I live my life with a lot of privilege. If I don't recognize my status and actively listen to the experiences of people of color, the LGBTQIA community, and women, I inadvertently perpetuate the biases of a patriarchal system from which I personally benefit. I can fall prey to stereotypes about and mischaracterizations of people of color. The simple act of watching the news can marginalize people for viewers and perpetuate unconscious racism.

Personally, I've had my perspective widened by the popular podcast *Serial*. Season 1, which told the story of Adnan El-Sayed, brought to light challenges in our criminal justice system. But it was season 3 that really opened my eyes to how much change is necessary in how we prosecute crime in the United States. Season 3 reported on the largely unknown stories of people in my hometown of Cleveland, Ohio. *Serial* shined the spotlight on people whose lives have been completely disrupted by a criminal justice system that rarely takes into account the systemic reasons that people are convicted of crimes.

When I listened to season 3 of the podcast, I came to realize that law-and-order answers to questions about crime and punishment are woefully inadequate. Solutions like mandatory minimum sentences and putting more cops on the streets might actually be making things worse. As a parent of teenagers, I had resisted the decriminalization of marijuana until I learned how disproportionate penalties are for people of color. Mass incarceration, the school-to-prison pipeline, and the absence of quality legal representation are systemic problems; they require bold, progressive solutions that grow out of awareness on the part of privileged people. To paraphrase the Apostle Paul, how can they hear without a reporter?

Because of my privilege, I have the responsibility of finding news sources that tell stories outside of my own experience. I must wrestle with the perspectives they present and adjust my own beliefs about the world in response. How might my beliefs about Muslims change if I consumed news from Al-Jazeera? Would I think of Europe differently if I subscribed to the BBC online? Would my positions on poverty, criminal justice, and race be reshaped if I sought out the stories from journalists of color? And underlying these questions is the issue of how my positions were formed in the first place.

Josh and his team told the story of my campaign in a short documentary titled *True Believer*. I really loved the finished product, but it's far from the whole story. It pulled at a couple of important threads, yet so much more was happening both in what I experienced and how I felt. Media, in all its forms, are profoundly valuable because they can probe into a story, but for the whole story, you need to hear more than just one telling.

Like never before, the opportunity exists for us to consume news in a balanced way that broadens our perspective. We are without excuse if we remain in our echo chambers, unaware of our own confirmation bias. Since objectivity is a myth and no media outlet can be relied upon to present the whole story, it is incumbent upon all of us as media consumers to actively seek out news stories that challenge our assumptions and make us think of things from a different perspective.

7

House Parties

★ ★ ★

Curing Political Cynicism

Scott and I have been politically engaged for as long as we can remember. Countless times, he and I had talked about politics over cigars and beer on my back porch. We often discussed how things needed to change but easily fell into a hopeless cynicism about the whole political system. I don't think we were all that different from many people who pay attention to politics. But now that we weren't just Monday-morning quarterbacks—we were actually in the game—we learned very quickly that having a political opinion is very different from organizing a campaign. We were both novices, and I often joked that we were making it up as we went along. Perhaps the most consequential idea we employed was holding as many house parties as possible.

We thought that our best chance to convince voters of my case was to go directly to them, introduce me as a congressional candidate, and share my vision. We asked supporters to invite their friends to hear me talk and answer their questions. We ended up doing scores of house parties throughout 2017 and 2018. For weeks on end, several of my evenings or Saturday afternoons would be filled up with these intimate events in the homes of friends and strangers.

Some of the house parties were small, just a couple of people. Only one of them had nobody show up, much to the dismay of our gracious host. We ended up doing a live Facebook conversation to try to connect with her friends who didn't show up that night. Most of the house parties had a dozen or so people, whom I always made sure I thanked for sacrificing a few hours on a weekday evening to talk politics instead of watching their favorite show on television.

In truth, the house parties were not always easy for me. I've long described myself as an antisocial extrovert. I like a party, but I prefer to sit at the edges cracking wise with a friend or two. This was clearly not an option when the purpose of the party was for voters and me to get to know each other. I forced myself to make small talk, shake hands, and mingle. When it was time for me to step forward and talk, I always breathed a sigh of relief. After years of preaching, giving a talk to a room of people felt most natural.

At each house party, I started with my stump speech: a ten- or fifteen-minute recitation of what motivated me to run for Congress, why Representative Womack needed to be replaced, and the policies I would advocate for in office. The speech I gave so many times varied very little from the one I developed at Congress Camp, and because of my message discipline, I was able to recite it time and time again. After hearing it for what seemed like the hundredth time, Scott and Vanessa would complain that they had grown bored with it, but I was able to stay on message.

I would explain to people that I am the kind of person who loves big ideas that are daring enough that they just might happen. I would tell them the story of starting Vintage Fellowship as an example of doing something daring and then transition into how electing a Brand New Congress was the big idea that had captured my imagination. I explained how I didn't think Congressman Womack was a very good representative for the people of Arkansas, but that I was committed to be their voice in Washington because I didn't take any donations from corporate political action committees. I would mention the big issues that mattered to me, like health care and immigration, but I usually left the policy details for the question-and-answer time. I always ended by asking the guests to do what I was doing—put people ahead of party—by donating, volunteering, and voting for my campaign.

At two different house parties, women who attended ended up deciding to run for office as well. They both ran for seats in our state legislature, advocating for progressive values that aligned with mine. During the campaign, I also met a third woman who was running. Her husband told me that they had heard me on a podcast and were inspired by what I was trying to do. On Election Day, when two of them were elected to the Arkansas state legislature, I could not have been prouder.

No matter how tired I was or how antisocial I felt at the beginning of a house party, I never regretted doing one, regardless of its size or how many people wrote a check to my campaign or signed up to volunteer. The opportunity to talk face-to-face with people throughout my district always gave me the energy to persevere in the hard work of campaigning, and I was often moved by the stories I heard.

Near the end of one party, a woman asked if she could chat with me for a few minutes. Through tears she shared that she and her husband didn't have health insurance. The plan offered through her husband's work was too expensive to be practical, and her part-time job didn't offer it. They made too much money to qualify for our state's insurance program for their kids, and so they gambled by going without.

During a track meet, her daughter who was in junior high fell and broke her leg. A couple of days later, she developed a blood infection. The cost of her treatment was astronomical. The doctors' offices were beginning to require them to pay for follow-up visits before her daughter would be seen for an appointment. With tears streaming down her cheeks, she told me about the agony of having to choose between making their mortgage payment or paying for the antibiotics her daughter needed to live.

"This is why we need universal health care," she said. "You're the first politician I've met who is talking about what my family needs. Please tell everyone you meet our story. This is why you've got to win."

I promised her that I would share her story and that I would fight for her family. That mom was not unique in wanting to be heard and needing to hear that someone would be her advocate in Washington on the issues that affected her family.

At another house party, a marketing manager named Ryan and his friend David cornered me. They wanted to talk about how disillusioned they felt after Bernie Sanders lost to Hillary Clinton, only to see her lose to Donald Trump. As millennial professionals, they felt like their generation was being ignored and taken for granted by the political establishment. Their concerns were being drowned out by special-interest groups and corporate donors who seemed to own the political process. Ryan and David wanted to be involved, but they had no idea if they could actually make a difference. I knew just how they felt.

One house party was hosted at a coffee shop by the leaders of Arkansas's Green Party. Scott and I drove two and a half hours to be there, wondering the whole way if anyone would actually show up to meet me, given my party affiliation. When I began my talk, I joked about how I was probably the first Republican to address a gathering of the Green Party, evidence that we are indeed living in strange political times. There was a lot of nervous laughter among the fifteen people who came. When I shared my ideas about how we could address climate change through bold progressive initiatives that even Republicans could support, I watched them glance at each other with unexpected smiles.

Two house parties were hosted by my friend Cara and her husband, Phillip, at their beautiful home. They are both doctors. At both events, Cara explained to her friends that as a doctor she had firsthand experience with the bureaucracy of health insurance companies. She was convinced to cross party lines and support a Republican for Congress because I was publicly advocating for a single-payer health-care system, which she believed would improve the care she gives her patients. She urged her skeptical Democratic friends to listen to me because I might just surprise them. I wish Cara could have introduced me at every house party! I talked to parents who feared for their children's safety at school. I heard the stories of millennial evangelicals who were serving refugees and the disadvantaged. Scientists pitched me ideas about how to address climate change. Senior citizens openly worried about the culture of the country they were leaving behind for future generations. Young professionals described the crushing load of their student debt. Every issue that ranks on a poll as a concern for voters became a real-life story for me as I sat in someone's living room while people told me about their lives.

Every single house party included frank conversation about the problems people in my district and across the country are facing. We didn't sugarcoat anything, but our conversations never devolved into sniping or finger-pointing. These personal exchanges felt so much more hopeful than the interactions that typically occur on social media. None of us were trying to score political points. We were listening to each other, grappling with the problems, and hashing out together how we could make things better. I was inspired by the guests' enthusiasm and passion. I learned from their perspectives and ideas about what would make a difference in people's lives.

Politics can make people cynical, which is completely understandable. In every election season, we are told that *this* election is the most important one of our lifetimes, which logically can't be true and sounds hollow after we hear it during every cycle. We're told that if we elect leaders from one party or the other, they'll solve the problems we face as a country, but rarely are these issues ever actually addressed. After hopes are dashed and expectations are unmet, one election after another, a large portion of Americans simply want no part in politics. Not surprisingly, they're turned off and tuned out.

Sometimes this cynicism is directed at politicians specifically. At several house parties, I was asked how the group could know that I could be trusted. "Politicians always say what people want to hear," someone would venture. "How can we be sure that you won't go to Washington and be corrupted like all the rest?" People expect politicians to double-cross them.

Decades of conservative rhetoric are partly to blame for this condition. Conservatives love to point out how Big Government is the enemy of the people, and when people see career politicians getting richer and richer while the average American family continues to struggle, it's easy to believe. I think negative campaign advertising is to blame as well. Campaigns are open season for stoking distrust in our leaders, and such images are hard to overcome when the campaigns end and the governing begins.

Some people direct their cynicism at the system itself: the process is the problem. I remember conversations with Vanessa over the years about how disheartening it is to feel like a single vote doesn't matter in the grand scheme of things. The process seems set on devouring good people and forcing them into the unfortunate mold of crooked politicians.

At one house party, I met a lady named Sherry who ended up becoming a friend. Sherry liked what she heard at the event she attended but wanted to get to know me better before hosting her own gathering. When we met for coffee the next week, she got right to the point. "You're running against your own party. If you win, you're just going to be one person who has no friends in DC. What difference can you really make?"

Sherry's skepticism didn't bother me. I told her that I understood her doubts and fears, but that one of the things that initially drew me to Brand New Congress was the idea that I would be part of a team.

"We'll see," she said, and then she agreed to host a house party for my campaign.

Sometimes people direct their cynicism at each other. All the members of one party or the other are lumped together and painted with the same unflattering brush. Republican voters are all racists or rednecks, Democratic voters are all freeloaders or elitists, and all voters look down on the people who don't vote. Labels like "libtard" and "deplorables" are used so frequently that people begin to dehumanize one another, seeing each other not as fellow citizens who simply have a different perspective on how to solve our common problems but as enemies who need to be defeated and shamed in the process.

It is not an original observation that we seem more divided now than we have been during my lifetime. Blaming social media and the cable news networks for this division is easy, but assigning blame doesn't help us move beyond it. Family dinners, workplaces, and worship gatherings are all political minefields where one comment can set off an explosion of arguments with lasting collateral damage.

Pastoring a church in the Trump era is exceedingly difficult. About 81 percent of white evangelicals voted for the president. Mainline churches, which have a reputation for being more liberal, still had 50 percent of their membership vote for Trump. The same is true of Catholics.

People can't just check their cynicism at the church door. The divisions and distrust that congregation members absorb and apply throughout the week have a way of seeping into the life of the church as well. At Vintage Fellowship, we don't talk partisan politics in our worship gatherings, but even so, after the 2016 presidential election, we sadly lost a couple of Trump voters because they no longer felt welcome in our congregation, where most people voted differently. The cynicism was inescapable.

I believe that cynicism is the fruit of fear. People become cynical when they are scared of being disappointed, lied to, or let down. Voters feel so repeatedly burned by politicians and the process that they are suspicious of anyone who is involved with politics. Cynicism is a self-protective impulse. People don't like to feel disappointed.

Ultimately, cynicism sets in when people are afraid to make themselves vulnerable again. Vulnerability opens us up to being hurt. When we go public with our beliefs and opinions, we become targets for criticism, whether on Facebook or in face-to-face conversations. Our motives can be called into question, and untrue and unfair assumptions can be made. Misunderstandings and mischaracterizations happen all too easily.

Every time I stood before a group of voters at a house party, I knew that I was talking to some skeptics and cynics. I was offering myself up to them for judgment. Every house party was an exercise in bravery, not just for me but also for those who dared to believe in the vision I was sharing.

Brené Brown has written much about vulnerability and bravery. She often quotes Teddy Roosevelt, himself a progressive Republican:

> It is not the critic who counts; not the man who points out how the strong man stumbles, or where the doer of deeds could have done them better. The credit belongs to the man who is actually in the arena, whose face is marred by dust and sweat and blood; who strives valiantly; who errs, who comes short again and again, because there is no effort without error and shortcoming; but who does actually strive to do the deeds; who knows great enthusiasms, the great devotions; who spends himself in a worthy cause; who at the best knows in the end the triumph of high achievement, and who at the worst, if he fails, at least fails while daring greatly, so that his place shall never be with those cold and timid souls who neither know victory nor defeat.[3]

At each and every house party, I found that the critics, skeptics, and cynics were far fewer than I had imagined. What I discovered is that, throughout Arkansas's Third District, countless people are creatively and positively engaged in trying to make their communities and country a more just and generous place. In their workplaces, churches, families, and organizations, they are in the arena.

The purpose of house parties was for voters to get to know me, which then translated into donations, volunteers, and support. They responded to a candidate who didn't pretend to have all the answers, who was willing to listen, and who had a fresh and compelling plan to actually address the problems they face. Voters want, and I believe deserve, to have a voice in the process. For many, my campaign gave them hope. More than once, voters told me that I would be the first Republican they would vote for in decades, or that I was the first candidate ever to whom they donated money.

I felt the gravity of their trust in me. They were taking a risk that I might actually put them ahead of the political establishment and petty partisan politics. They were placing their hope in me, which was most humbling.

I think the lasting impact of our house parties is the one voters had on me. Campaigning for Congress didn't make me cynical. It fueled my hope, as over and over again I met people who unselfishly give of themselves for the sake of others. They are paying attention. They have ideas. They are doing in small and big ways whatever they can to live out the promise of America.

The cure for cynicism is creative engagement in a difficult process for the good of others. During my campaign, I met people who are in the arena daily, daring greatly. They gave me—and still give me—the encouragement and energy to persevere.

8

Follow the Money

★ ★ ★

Treating the Symptoms
and Ignoring the Disease

At the beginning of my campaign, when I was asked what issues mattered most to me, I consistently answered that I was running for Congress because I believe all Americans deserve health care, because I believe America should be a country that is welcoming of immigrants and refugees, and because I believe we need a tax system that is fair to the American people and doesn't allow the biggest corporations in the country to get away with not paying any taxes.

At the end of my campaign, when asked what issues mattered most to me, I had one simple answer: the way we fund our political campaigns. In fact, I have become convinced that unless we overhaul campaign finance, it is very unlikely we'll ever be able to solve the other biggest problems we face as a country.

According to the Center for Responsive Politics, $5.2 billion was spent on the midterm elections in 2018.[4] The average successful congressional campaign now spends well north of a million dollars. This astronomical amount of money pays for political advertising of all kinds; pays the salaries of campaign staff; buys technology, equipment, and supplies needed in campaign offices; and makes it possible for candidates to travel all over their districts. Some of the money also goes to getting candidates' names on the ballot.

To run for office, a person has to fill out paperwork and jump through some hoops to qualify to be on the ballot. The requirements are far from standardized across the country. Some states mandate that candidates collect a certain number of signatures from registered voters to qualify, demonstrating at least a modicum of public support for the candidacy. Many other states require the candidate to pay a filing fee. Typically, that filing fee is 1 percent of the salary of the desired office, paid to the secretary of state's office in that state. For congressional races, most candidates pay $1,750 in filing fees to run. Three states, however, allow the political parties in those states to set the filing fee. My state, Arkansas, is one of those states.

Candidates running for Congress in Georgia have to pay $5,000 to place their names on the ballot. Florida has a filing fee of $10,600, but candidates there can collect signatures in lieu of the fee. In 2018, the filing fee to run for Congress as a Republican in Arkansas was $15,000, by far the highest in the entire country. In other words, no candidate for the U.S. Congress paid more to have his or her name on the ballot in 2018 than I did.

Arkansas is a bright-red state, typically rewarding the Republican nominee for president with one of the highest winning percentages in the country, but it has not always been this way. Arkansas famously gave the country President Bill Clinton and some Democratic senators over the years, but recently the state has become solidly Republican. People often ask me why the Republican Party in Arkansas is so strong and why the Democratic Party in the state seems so weak. In response, I refer them to the presidential primary of 2016.

In 2016 the Arkansas Democratic Party had a presidential filing fee of $2,500; as a result, after Hillary Clinton, Bernie Sanders, and four other also-rans paid the fee, the Arkansas Democrats added $15,000 to their bank account. The Republican primary had thirteen candidates, each paying $25,000 to qualify. The Arkansas Republican Party (called Arkansas GOP, or ARGOP) added $325,000 to its coffers from the presidential election alone. This huge difference means that ARGOP has far more money to spend on staff, support, and advertising for its candidates. Recognizing this difference, the Arkansas Democrats have begun raising their own filing fees, setting off a campaign finance arms race in my state.

A former Arkansas Republican legislator tweeted in early 2018 that he was a part of the committee that set the fees and that its stated purpose was to make it more difficult for Republican incumbents to be challenged in primary races. In other words, the party establishment wants to make it as difficult as possible for regular people to run for office on the Republican ticket so that existing elected officials can keep their seats.[5]

Sadly, the Arkansas GOP is not alone in trying to protect incumbents. Gerrymandering is the most common tool of incumbent protection. By drawing the lines of congressional districts, state legislatures protect the seats they already control by making it impossible for someone from another party to win. It has the effect of allowing politicians to pick their voters rather than voters picking their leaders. In a few states—including Pennsylvania, Ohio, and North Carolina—federal courts have thrown out the gerrymandered districts and are requiring use of a fairer system.

In New York, the 2018 primaries for different offices are held on different days. If you lived in New York City, for instance, you might go on one day to vote in your congressional primary and then have to go back to the polls three weeks later to vote in your gubernatorial primary. This made voting more complicated, confusing voters and thus driving down turnout. The calculation was that a convoluted system benefits incumbents.

One of my Brand New Congress slatemates, Anthony Clark, ran against an incumbent congressman in Illinois. Anthony and his team diligently worked to collect the necessary signatures to qualify for the ballot, only to have their efforts undermined when his opponent challenged the signatures in court. Even though the signatures were valid and his name was eventually put on the ballot, Anthony was forced to waste precious time, energy, and money in an unnecessary court battle. Dirty tricks like this are all too common on both sides of the aisle.

I discovered in campaigning that most people have a sense that the system is somehow rigged, but very few actually understand how.

I turned forty-three years old on January 8, 2018, and decided to use my birthday for a fund-raising event. In essence, I threw myself a party and asked my friends to pay to come to it. Right before they sang to me and we cut the cake, I thanked my friends for coming and then told the assembled crowd that their donations that night were going to help me pay to get my name on the ballot. When I said that the fee was fifteen thousand dollars, there was an audible gasp in the room. People simply had no idea what it actually costs to run for office.

The outrageous cost of political campaigns is not a problem, however, for candidates who accept money from corporate political action committees (PACs). While the federal limit in 2018 for individuals' donations to a candidate was twenty-seven hundred dollars per election, PACs could donate five thousand dollars per election. Most incumbents spend time courting corporate PAC donors and being courted by them. My opponent, Steve Womack, had over a million dollars in his campaign war chest before our campaign even started, the vast majority of which came not from small-dollar donors but from corporate PACs and their representatives.

Corporate PACs are not the only problem. So-called Super-PACs have no limit on what they can collect and spend on behalf of a candidate, as long as they don't coordinate directly with the campaign. People like the Koch brothers and George Soros gain political influence by setting up SuperPACs and investing in the candidates they believe will do their bidding when in office. Wealthy evangelicals have also recognized the opportunity afforded by SuperPACs and have funneled tens of millions of dollars into them to influence elections in recent years.

All Brand New Congress candidates, myself included, agreed

on principle that big corporations and special-interest groups have an outsized influence on our political system because of how campaigns are financed. We each pledged to put the needs of people first by refusing SuperPAC support and corporate PAC money. We relied completely on the small-dollar donations of regular working people across the country who believed in what we were trying to accomplish.

But even that was more difficult for me. When Brand New Congress launched, they used a donation platform called Act-Blue. ActBlue was set up to make it easier for Democratic candidates to crowdsource their campaigns by collecting money from small-dollar donors. Even though they publicly advocate for progressive policies such as universal health care and combating climate change, ActBlue refused to let me use their platform simply because I was not a Democrat. While it is well within their prerogative to make decisions about how to run their business, ActBlue's policy kept me from being able to benefit from tandem fund-raisers for BNC's candidates.

The workaround that we used was a different crowdsourcing platform called CrowdPac. Its user base is much smaller than ActBlue, but it enabled me to collect the donations I needed to run my campaign. However, with only a few precious weeks left before my primary date, the CrowdPac board of directors fired its founder for his public support of President Trump and suspended the accounts of all Republicans using the platform. At the most critical juncture, I had to spend time and resources proving to CrowdPac that I opposed the president's agenda in order to have my fund-raising restored.

Money in politics is a problem.

The travails of raising enough money to qualify to be on the ballot and to run my campaign forced me to think a lot about how campaigns are funded. I realized for the first time that all of the issues I care about are symptoms of our campaign finance system. That system is actually the disease.

The ultimate loyalty of elected officials is not to the people who vote for them but to those corporate PACs and special-interest groups that actually fund their campaigns. Even though polling shows broad consensus on many issues facing the nation, progress is actually impeded because if our elected leaders were to act on those issues in accordance with voters' wishes, the officeholders would have to defy the entities that helped get them elected.

For instance, the majority of Americans, including Republicans, support overhauling our health-care system by implementing Medicare for All. However, elected officials on both sides of the aisle refuse to enact this reform because the pharmaceutical and insurance companies that donate millions of dollars to their campaigns oppose it.

Increasing the military budget seems to be the only thing in Washington that has bipartisan support. We spend more on defense than the next thirteen countries in the world combined, yet every year Congress overwhelmingly votes to spend more. I believe this happens because defense contractors invest millions of dollars ensuring the reelection of Republican and Democratic incumbents.

The same is true on just about every issue—from gun reform to climate change, from agriculture to tax reform.

When I dug more into this issue, I was most surprised to learn how campaign finance even impacts immigration reform. Our current immigration system makes it very difficult for people to enter our country with proper documentation. As a result, millions of people have immigrated without this documentation. When they are caught by Immigration and Customs Enforcement (ICE), they are placed in detention centers. Congress requires ICE to keep its detention centers at at least 90 percent capacity to retain its funding from the federal government. ICE agents thus have a monetary motivation to detain undocumented people. Nine of the ten largest ICE detention centers in the United States are operated by three for-profit prison companies that have received federal contracts. Those three for-profit prison companies have donated millions of dollars to the campaigns of the very congresspeople who wrote and passed these regulations.

Not only policy is shaped by the influence of big money, so are the political parties. Both parties want congresspeople to spend hours each day calling wealthy corporate donors, trying to raise money, not just for themselves but also for their party and its affiliates. People have asked me how it is possible for a freshman congresswoman like Alexandria Ocasio-Cortez to be so well-prepared in committee hearings. The answer I always give is that since she is not like every other representative, who is dependent on corporate donors and therefore spending 70 percent of his or her time fund-raising, she actually has time to be prepared to do her job.

A congressperson who can raise a lot of money for the party is likely to get plum committee assignments in the House of Representatives. In January 2018, Congressman Womack became chair of the Budget Committee, a powerful and coveted position. A Politico article at the time suggested that he didn't win this privilege based on seniority or expertise. Rather, he had raised more money for the Republican Party than anyone else who was up for the seat.[6] Essentially, using big-money campaign donations, Congressman Womack bought himself the chair of a committee.

If you want to understand why your representatives aren't taking action on the issues that matter most to you, follow the money.

With a much better understanding of how campaign finance actually works and its impact on our system, I began to emphasize to voters in my district that this is the single most important issue we face as a country. Unless we take specific steps, the loyalty of our leaders will never be with the voters and will remain with the corporations that fund their campaigns. I advocated to voters, and continue to do so, for the following three policies to be enacted.

First, we need to publicly fund elections. As long as the primary source of funding of political campaigns is corporate PACs and special-interest groups, the will of the people will be subjugated. Some Democrats and Republicans alike who have recognized the campaign finance crisis have suggested that a tax credit of up to two hundred dollars per person for donations to campaigns would radically increase the number of people who participate in the election process through donating. Since politicians have proven that their loyalty is with those who fund their campaigns, we need to make sure that those funders are the American people rather than corporations.

Second, we need to limit campaign spending. Since the government has already limited what individuals can donate to a candidate, I believe it would be wise to also limit what those candidates can spend. Limiting spending levels the playing field for grassroots campaigns challenging incumbents and decreases the need for politicians to amass huge war chests from corporate donors. It also makes it so that people who run for office don't have to be independently wealthy to do so. This reform would also have the welcome by-product of shortening our now-perpetual election season, since candidates would need to save their money to spend it when it would have the most impact—close to Election Day. Granted, if we were to limit campaign spending, consultants and lobbyists would have to find jobs somewhere other than the political industrial complex, but the overall benefits far outweigh this inconvenience.

Third, we need to repeal *Citizens United*. In 2010, the Supreme Court ruled in a case called *Citizens United v. the FEC* that political spending on behalf of a candidate by corporations is protected speech and therefore cannot be restricted by the federal government. This opened the floodgates of SuperPAC money into our system and changed American politics. The reality is that corporations are not people with constitutional protections. In all likelihood, overturning *Citizens United* would require an amendment to the Constitution, but given the crisis to our democracy caused by unfettered corporate spending, such a drastic step is not only prudent but necessary.

While I fully believe these proposals are necessary, I have very little hope that the politicians who benefit from the current system will ever enact the changes. But we don't have to wait for politicians to lead on campaign finance reform. This is one area where we the people have far more power than we realize.

If a majority of Americans wake up to the reality of how big money has corrupted our system and our leaders in the process, and if a majority of Americans made a commitment to simply refuse to vote for any politician, regardless of party affiliation, who takes money from corporate PACs, enough pressure would be exerted on candidates to swear off corporate money. A *Wall Street Journal* / NBC poll in 2016 showed that the leading issue for voters was that wealthy donors and corporations have too much influence over who wins our elections. A consensus is growing, and politicians are taking notice. Several candidates for president in 2020 have recognized this trend and made a pledge not to take corporate PAC money. We need to keep the pressure on politicians until the idea of taking corporate money becomes a debilitating liability for all candidates for office.

As a person of faith and a pastor, I can't help but think about the life and example of Jesus when I'm considering issues. When I read the Gospels, I find a Jesus who was deeply suspicious of those who used wealth to gain influence. He refused to give preferential treatment to the rich and well-connected. He consistently sided with the poor and oppressed and denounced the powerful. Jesus said in Matthew 6:24 that it is impossible to serve both God and money. I believe it is also impossible to serve both money and the needs of people.

It is a moral imperative for people who follow the example and teachings of Jesus to work toward America having a political system that protects every person's right to participate in the process, ensures that no person is disenfranchised, and doesn't value corporate donors and political lobbyists more highly than average citizens.

For me, the deadline to file with the Arkansas secretary of state was May 1, 2018. On that morning, Calvin, Scott, and I, with the documentary crew in tow, made the three-and-a-half-hour drive to Little Rock so that I could officially register my campaign. We walked into the rotunda of the capitol and found a series of tables set up that I had to visit in succession. The first place I went was to the ARGOP table. After shaking hands with the state party chair, I sat at the table and filled out some paperwork. When I finished, the clerk said matter-of-factly, "That will be fifteen thousand dollars."

As I pulled out my checkbook to write the biggest single check I had ever written in my life, I noticed some signage on the table. In a clear plastic holder, a printed piece of paper listed the cost of running for each respective office in 2018 in Arkansas. It reminded me of a church bake sale where one might read that a slice of apple pie cost three dollars or chocolate chip cookies were three for five dollars.

"U.S. Congress: $15,000."

With gratitude for the hundreds of people who had made small-dollar donations because they believed in my campaign, I committed myself to be their voice should I make it to Washington and to never become a politician who could be bought and sold. And then I wrote the fifteen-thousand-dollar check.

9

Being a Bivocational Candidate

★ ★ ★

The Challenge of "Regular People"
Running for Office

When Vanessa and I moved our family to Arkansas to start Vintage Fellowship in 2006, we left behind the denomination we grew up in and our entire support network. After pastoring in our denomination for a decade, the faith shift we experienced meant we couldn't stay where we were—geographically or theologically. Our friends and colleagues had no desire to support our effort to start a progressive evangelical church where people could express their doubts about conservative doctrine, everyone would be accepted without judgment, and those with bad church experiences would be cared for instead of shamed. In our minds, the chance to follow our dreams outweighed the risk of going it alone.

Many church planters get financial support from their denominations or from mother churches who nurture the new church for a few years while it gets its footing. Our denomination wanted nothing to do with us, and we could not find a progressive evangelical church to help us. We were forced to do whatever it took to launch Vintage Fellowship.

To pay the bills, I found two jobs that allowed me to devote my spare time to starting the church. During the week, I taught fourth grade at a small Christian school, and in the evenings and on Saturdays, I worked at a Christian bookstore. It was utterly exhausting, but we felt the sacrifice was worth it. After about ten months, I was hired by a local textbook company, which simplified my life some, but I still had the pressure of being a bivocational pastor.

Over the past twelve years, my career path has been a winding one, affording me the opportunity to work in different industries from digital education to advertising sales to the very unique field of shopper marketing, which analyzes consumer behavior in stores like Walmart (headquartered in my district). Throughout, I have remained a bivocational pastor. At times, I've been content with that, but at most times, I have not. If someone had told me when we started Vintage that twelve years later, I would still be bivocational, I'm not sure I would have done it.

After five years of carrying the dual loads of a day job and pastoring a church, I hit a breaking point. Within a six-week period of time, I experienced two panic attacks. The pressure was getting to me, and I wasn't okay. Vanessa and I decided to start going to therapy to see if talking to a professional could help me get a better handle on my life. At one particularly insightful therapy appointment, I was complaining to my therapist that I didn't want to be bivocational anymore, and I wasn't sure if I could continue.

In response, he asked, "Robb, do you want to pastor or do you want to pastor Vintage?"

I thought carefully about what he was asking. Was it the work of pastoring that I loved most, which I could do in any context, including one that could pay me enough to do it exclusively, or was it pastoring the rare community of Vintage Fellowship that I loved most?

I answered honestly, "I want to pastor Vintage."

"Well, you're doing that," he replied.

Those words unlocked a door and ushered me into a new era in my life. I realized that I was doing what I wanted to do. Yes, having a day job added additional pressure, but it also made it possible for me to do what I loved. If I could find some kind of internal contentment with my situation, it would free me up mentally, emotionally, and spiritually to remember that the life I wanted to live was not out in the future but was actually my present reality.

Around this same time, Vanessa read *Big Magic* by Elizabeth Gilbert. She told me about how Gilbert describes the tension that happens when an artist has to be financially supported by their art. It can commercialize the art and suck the joy out of it. Gilbert's advice is for artists to keep working so that they can be free to create the art they want to create. Vanessa and I talked about how Vintage was our art, about how free we were to experiment and try things other pastors might be afraid to attempt, all because we didn't put pressure on Vintage to pay all of our bills. I was finally becoming comfortable with being bivocational.

Because of my experience as a bivocational pastor, when Brand New Congress pitched a vision of everyday working people running for office, I already had a sense of how that might work. I would have a day job to pay the bills, but on weekends and in the evenings, I would throw myself into a passion project, the thing I really believed in, the dream that lit me up inside. Because Vanessa had been ordained and was taking on more leadership at Vintage, I was able to have the bandwidth to run for office.

A typical day in the life of a bivocational candidate is very full. I would get up in the morning and help get the kids off to school. Before heading out the door, I would schedule social media posts for the day and answer a few campaign e-mails. Once I was at work, I would use my lunch hour and other breaks to catch up on the news of the day, seeing if there was anything I needed to respond to. I'd use my time in the car to call Scott, my campaign manager, and review what was happening with the campaign. Most evenings, I would hurry through dinner with the family before heading out to a house party. Often, my days ended late with more e-mails and messages to campaign volunteers.

Running an effective campaign is about more than just being able to talk compellingly about the issues or tell an engaging personal story. It also requires a high level of organization. We had to recruit, train, and rely on volunteers to knock on doors, make phone calls, and promote the campaign on social media and real life. We had to manage a full calendar of events. We had to be responsive to press inquiries. I've always prided myself in my ability to be productive and efficient. I've always said that I'm at my best when my plate is full. But running for office, pastoring a church, and working a job was pushing me to my limits. I had no shortage of anxious thoughts to process with Vanessa and our therapist. Being bivocational meant juggling what actually amounted to three full-time jobs at the same time. One could even say I was "trivocational" during the campaign.

What I didn't anticipate was there being vocational volatility during the campaign. When I launched the campaign, I was working for a shopper marketing technology company out of Vancouver, British Columbia, trying to break open the Walmart market in Bentonville, Arkansas, for them. My boss was supportive of my run for Congress, but six months in, he and I began having some hard conversations. Sales weren't coming as fast as we had hoped. The company was beginning to run low on its funding and was struggling to raise more money. It was considering a pivot to an approach that would make my job obsolete. In September 2017, we had the hardest conversation of all, in which we decided it was time to cut ties.

On one hand, I was relieved because my day job hadn't been easy. The pressure of knowing the company's future depended on my performance weighed heavily on me. I was glad to have it released. But it was replaced by a new pressure of how we were going to pay the bills while maintaining the responsibilities of leading a church and running a campaign. I didn't know how I was going to provide for my family while also being free to be an effective candidate.

I did a short-term gig with a local marketing agency as a commission-only salesperson that didn't produce much at all, until the day a friend called. He was the sales manager at our cable company. We had worked together a few years previously at one of the television stations in the area. During that time, we had grown very close, and he really wanted me to join his team of advertising salespeople. He told me that he had received approval to hire me, despite the fact that I was a candidate for Congress. Because of our friendship, he said that he understood he might not be getting 100 percent of me, but he still wanted me on his team. In January 2018, I started.

Less than two months later, I was sitting at my desk on a Thursday morning when my phone rang.

"Robb, this is Mark from human resources. Do you have a minute to talk?" I had never spoken to Mark before.

"Sure," I replied.

"Robb, are you running for office?"

"Yes, I'm running for Congress."

"Do you know that our company has a policy that an employee cannot be a candidate for office?"

I swallowed hard. "Yes, but when I was hired a couple months ago, I was told that an exception was being made for me."

"Well, I'll have to look into that. I am not aware that an exception was made."

When we hung up, I sat at my desk in stunned silence. *Here we go again,* I thought.

I packed up my coffee mug and a few other personal items and drove home. I just knew that I wouldn't be going back to work there.

As I drove home, I noticed that on the roads around the cable company's office were several of my campaign signs. Volunteers had placed them there that very week. As I tried to piece together what happened, I imagined that someone at my office saw the signs, realized I was running for office, knew the company policy, and made a call to HR. I wasn't angry with whoever connected the dots; I was happy that the campaign signs were getting noticed.

It turned out that whoever gave the green light to hiring me despite my campaign didn't have the authority to make that decision. HR was not going to make an exception for me, and I was forced to resign. In my final call with Mark from HR, I told him that I never hid the fact that I was running. Name recognition is kind of important to campaigns. "Running for Congress is not something you do in private," I joked. He laughed and apologized for what had happened. I appreciated his apology, but I immediately began worrying once again about how we were going to make it financially.

In addition to our finances, my other biggest concern was health care for our family. When I worked for the start-up, we had purchased our health insurance through the marketplace created by the Affordable Care Act. Having employer-provided health coverage for a few months was a welcome respite, but with that job going away, we'd have to return to the exchange for our health coverage, this time with much less financial security. I imagined how many other families throughout my district and across the country were thrust into the same kind of uncertainty about health insurance when unexpected job changes happen. I doubled down on my commitment to advocate for a better system for all of these families, including my own, even while I internally wondered if this huge headache was worth being a politician.

"Career politicians" is a phrase that is often used derisively of people who have been in office for decades. I used it countless times to describe my opponent and the establishment politicians who seem so very out of touch with everyday Americans. The typical career path for someone who wants to be in politics is to run for a local office such as school board or city council. In time, they may be able to graduate to mayor or state legislator. If they wait their turn and stand in line, eventually a federal position in the House of Representatives or even the Senate might open up.

This typical progression of political advancement almost played out in my campaign. In late 2017, President Trump and Secretary of State Rex Tillerson were having a public spat about Tillerson's performance. Pundits speculated that if Tillerson resigned, CIA director Mike Pompeo was likely to take over at State. If that happened, Senator Tom Cotton from Arkansas was on the short list to become CIA director. A spokesman for my opponent told the press that Congressman Womack would be interested in the potential Senate opening.

If all of these dominoes were to fall, it would radically alter the race I was in for Arkansas's Third District seat. Scott and I ran through the various scenarios. Who would our opponents be should the seat be vacant? How would that impact our campaign? After a long conversation, I said, "Let's just pause for a minute. Can you believe we're actually discussing how who the U.S. secretary of state is directly impacts my life?" We sat for a few minutes in bemused silence, soaking in the bizarreness of it all.

What I was trying to do, along with all of my Brand New Congress slatemates, was jump the line. We were trying to upset the status quo by giving voters the option of casting their ballot for someone whose life experience more closely resembles their own. The presupposition we were operating under was that teachers, scientists, bartenders, and pastors are actually better prepared to represent regular people in the halls of Congress than career politicians or self-financed millionaires and billionaires. Rather than waiting in line for our turn to come, we were elbowing our way to the front, convinced that regular people deserve someone who would look out for their interests.

I wasn't the only BNC candidate to encounter job trouble while campaigning. Others were fired from their jobs or forced to take leaves of absence from their companies. The husband of one of our candidates was fired from his job because his employer didn't agree with his spouse's politics. Some candidates were forced to take out personal loans to support themselves during their campaigns. We were putting our own careers on the line to challenge the career politicians.

Several times during the course of the campaign, people would ask me if I supported term limits as a way of getting rid of career politicians. The rationale is that if we limit the number of terms a person can serve in Congress, we're more likely to

elect regular people to office. While I am obviously very sympathetic to the goal of electing regular people instead of career
politicians, I'm skeptical that term limits would actually produce better congresspeople.

My fear is that enacting term limits would have the unin-
tended consequence of giving more power to corporate donors
and their lobbyists. Under our current system of campaign
finance, term-limited races allow corporate donors to act as
kingmakers by putting their substantial contributions behind
the candidates of their choosing. Once elected, these inexpe-
rienced representatives would feel obligated to their donors,
allowing corporate lobbyists to exercise an undue influence
over legislation.

Rather than encouraging more regular people to run for
office, term limits in a vacuum would also make it more advan-
tageous for people who are independently wealthy to run for
office. Given the ungodly expense of most campaigns, term
limits, in my estimation, would widen the gap between the
rich and powerful and the vast majority of Americans. Term
limits seem to me like a policy that serves the oligarchy more
than democracy.

I would only support term limits as part of a broader
revamping of how our elections are financed. The way to break
the stranglehold that career politicians have over elected office
is to create a campaign finance system that levels the playing
field for everyone. Public financing of elections and limiting
campaign spending are the policies that would actually have
the intended impact of making it easier for working Americans
to run for office and be the representatives of other working
Americans in Washington.

Vanessa is a bivocational pastor too. She has worked as an artist
and entrepreneur for years. Her career has enabled her the flex-
ibility to both pastor and work from home so that she is very
available for our children. In mid-2017, she received an e-mail
from an agency looking for an artist who could do a major

mosaic installation at a newly constructed hotel. They wanted her to submit a proposal.

Providentially, her proposal was selected, and she began working on creating fourteen mosaic panels that would be installed as a twenty-five-foot wall in the main restaurant of the new hotel. They paid her half of her fee upfront and the other half upon completion. That first payment arrived in early 2018, right around the time Mark from HR was calling me to say I had to resign from my job.

Somehow, we discerned, God was involved in all of this. Rather than searching for a new job while speeding toward my primary date, we decided that I should campaign full-time while we lived off of her big mosaic project. For the final three months of my campaign, I was able to focus on knocking on doors, speaking to groups, attending house parties, and doing everything I could to get elected without the pressure of how we were going to pay the bills.

The hotel was set to be completed in the fall of 2018. Vanessa and I would have to travel to install her mosaic wall, which, as it turned out, was at a high-end hotel in Washington. One way or another, come November 2018, we were going to DC.

10

The Emotional Roller Coaster

★ ★ ★

How Authentic Do We
Want Our Politicians to Be?

Before I began my run for Congress, I received a lot of training from the Brand New Congress team. We talked about campaign structure, budgets, power maps, and field plans. I learned how to do call time for fund-raising and file reports with the Federal Election Commission. While I never felt like I had it all figured out, I was confident in my ability to put together a campaign. However, there was one aspect of campaigning that nobody prepared me for: the emotional roller coaster.

For the year and a half that I ran my congressional race, my emotions went through an unending series of high-speed curves and flips. I was constantly unnerved, unsettled, and uncomfortable. I rarely felt peaceful or calm. I also began to realize that any brief reprieve was probably just the anticipation of climbing the next hill that would send me plunging. I feared for the well-being of my family. I flirted with the joyful hope of winning. I worried about how I came off to the people with whom I interacted. I entertained the shame of thinking I was wasting everyone's time and money, not to mention my own.

As these feelings swirled within me, I never felt confident about how much of them to reveal. I would talk about them to Vanessa or Scott, but I didn't know if it would be appropriate to share them at a house party or with a voter. I wanted to be authentic, but how authentic is too authentic? Did voters want a politician who was honest about the issues or honest about everything? I really wasn't sure, but the campaign trail gave me lots of opportunities to live in the tension.

In the spring of 2017, I was finalizing my decision to run for Congress, going through Brand New Congress training, and putting the pieces of my campaign organization together. In the midst of all of that, one evening I received a phone call from the father of one of my daughter's friends. He called to tell Vanessa and me that Charleigh, our daughter, had texted his son some things that concerned him.

As he struggled to find the words, I felt time slow down. My mind raced.

What could be wrong? Was this going to be something disapproving about how we express our faith? Surely she didn't send him any inappropriate pictures.

Before my brain could settle on what I thought was the most likely explanation, he began to speak again.

"Charleigh sent him a text saying that she was thinking about killing herself," he said with his voice cracking.

Time stopped. I could feel my blood rush to my head. My ears began to ring. I remembered to breathe.

Through tears, this concerned dad told us how much he loved our daughter and how he hated to violate the trust between our kids. But he had discovered the text and was insistent that we know. Vanessa and I thanked him, and after hanging up the phone we just stared at each other for what felt like forever. When we composed ourselves, we went to Charleigh's room and began a conversation that continues to this day and probably will always go on.

Charleigh is our third kid. She joined our family when she was three and a half months old as a foster child. We adopted her when she was a year and a half old. When I started my campaign, she was thirteen years old. She has an infectious laugh and a scary mastery of meme culture, sings like an angel, and is unbelievably talented as a graphic artist. She's half Mexican and a quarter Cuban. She doesn't look like the rest of us, but our family would not be complete without her.

That winter, she had contracted mononucleosis. She spent weeks in bed and missed a lot of school. Her recovery had been slow, and she didn't seem herself. Vanessa and I assumed that she was still slowly getting back to normal that spring. We now realized that something else was actually happening.

The thought that she was so depressed and anxious that she would consider taking her own life shook me to my core. Vanessa and I told her about the phone call from her friend's dad and began to ask her about what was going on in her head and heart. It took a long time for her to begin to open up, and it would be a long time before we felt we were actually peeling back the layers of her feelings.

I don't think I slept that night.

The next day, I put the campaign on hold so that Vanessa and I could take Charleigh to a behavioral health facility to get an evaluation. They didn't suggest inpatient care for her but did recommend that we get Charleigh some additional professional help. We made an appointment with a therapist as soon as we could. We also got on the waiting list to see one of the two psychiatrists in our area who specialize in treating kids so that we could determine if she needed medication.

I remember sitting with Vanessa one day at lunch talking through the whole situation. I told her that we needed to prepare ourselves for the idea that she might not get better. This wasn't a cold that would go away in a few weeks. We needed to think of it as something chronic that would be with us—and her—for a long time. As that reality set in, we both felt the gravity of it, wondering aloud if we could carry this burden along with everything else that was going on in our lives.

"Is this my fault?" I asked Vanessa. "Have I put too much pressure on the family with this crazy idea of running for office?"

Vanessa didn't have the answer. Neither did I.

Finally, Vanessa spoke, "You're running because people need help. The politicians care more about their own power than they do solving problems. You've been talking about health care, especially getting better coverage for mental illness. Our kid needs that. Imagine all of the other kids out there who need it too. You've got to run to help them and their families."

I believed her.

Our sense that Charleigh's distress wasn't going to go away quickly was correct. In the ensuing months, she would experience new waves of anxiety. Therapy was beneficial, but it would take time for her to build trust with her therapist. We eventually had an appointment with the psychiatrist, who prescribed medication for Charleigh. It would take many more months before we found the drug and dosage that would make some kind of difference. In the meantime, our family would have to ride the onslaught of waves when they arrived.

In the fall of that year, Charleigh began to struggle again. It was late one night when the phone rang. Someone in our home had called the suicide prevention hotline. They triangulated the call, pinpointed our house, and called to alert someone else who was there. Vanessa and I ran up the stairs to Charleigh's room and found her in tears, huddled in the corner. We sat on the floor and held her.

Then our doorbell rang. I went downstairs to answer it and found a police officer on our doorstep. He had received a call from the hotline too and came over to see if everything was alright. I explained that we were with our daughter and that she was safe. He said he needed to come in to check on her.

I hesitated. I had no idea how Charleigh would respond to a uniformed stranger invading the privacy of her room. I imagined him spouting some meaningless platitudes and leaving thinking he had done something to make a difference. I wasn't so sure that was a good idea.

"My wife is up in her room with her now," I said. "She's been struggling for a while. She's seeing a therapist now and has started medication. I'm just not sure having a stranger come into her room is the best thing right now."

He took out his little notebook and said, "What's your daughter's name, if she is your daughter?"

What did he just say? I felt myself getting belligerent. I took a deep breath and said shortly, "Wait here. It might be better if you talk to my wife."

I closed the door and returned to Charleigh's room. I tried to explain to Vanessa that I wasn't going to let the police officer into our house, that I was starting to get angry with him, and that she better go to the door. I'm not sure she understood how upset the police officer made me, but we switched places. I held Charleigh in my arms and waited for Vanessa to return.

As I sat there holding my girl, whom I love with all of my life, all I could imagine were the headlines in the paper the next day: "Local Congressional Candidate Arrested for Assaulting a Police Officer." I laughed and cried.

There were many nights during the campaign that Vanessa and I would lay in bed and talk in the darkness.

"How did she do today?" I would ask.

"It was hard, but we got through it."

"I want you to know that I'll quit the whole thing tomorrow if we think it would make a difference. The only thing that matters to me is that my girl is okay. If this is too much, I'll quit the campaign tomorrow."

"I know," Vanessa would reply, "but I don't think that's necessary yet."

Thankfully, it never was necessary. But there was never a day throughout the campaign where I didn't consider shutting it all down. I would knock on doors, call voters, or make a speech at an event, and then as soon as it was over, I'd immediately go back to thinking about Charleigh. Very literally, her life was hanging in the balance, and every single day I worried that I was making the situation worse for her, not better.

And I worried about what impact I was having on my other children too. During the campaign, we took a few days off to take our eldest child to college. Matt had been accepted into one of the best (and most expensive) art schools in the country.

I was enormously proud, but I also knew that if I was focusing on campaigning, I couldn't focus on making a lot of money for tuition payments.

Calvin was a junior in high school during most of the campaign. When we started the campaign, he was shorter than me, but by the end, he was inches taller. He was growing up, coming into his own, finding his voice and passions. I worried that being away from home as much as I was meant that he didn't have his dad around enough at the very time he was becoming a man.

Our youngest, Whimsy, had been our surprise baby. We didn't plan her, but she joined our family around the time Vanessa and I were both turning forty. I often joked that having a baby in the house when you have teenagers makes it infinitely easier because there is always an extra set of hands to feed or change her and that you have built-in babysitters. But I also knew from experience that having a toddler is exhausting all by itself. I feared that I wasn't pulling my fair share of the parenting.

Running for office is an emotional roller coaster like nothing I have ever experienced. Between Charleigh's struggles, my anxiety about being a good dad, my job insecurity, and the busyness of campaigning, I lived with constant tension. At campaign events, I needed to project confidence and stability. I needed to show voters that I had the right combination of a grasp of the issues, empathy for their concerns, and the personal character that would make them trust me with their support. I instinctively knew that if I cracked under the pressure, it could hurt my campaign. I had to be honest, but I also had to hold it all together.

I found a lot of solace in the distraction of the actual work of campaigning. I spent a lot of time knocking on doors, introducing myself to voters, and asking for their support. Given my experience in sales, I wasn't intimidated by talking to strangers, but I was always sensitive to the reality that nobody likes to be interrupted by an unsolicited ring of their doorbell.

Canvassing neighborhoods, as it turned out, often brought some much-needed comic relief. One Saturday, I was knocking on doors in Rogers, the town that my opponent once served as mayor. It was about eleven in the morning when I climbed the front steps of a nice house. I was surprised to see the front door wide open. I crossed the porch and noted how well decorated the living room was. My eyes scanned the living room and then the kitchen. As I reached to ring the doorbell, I noticed a man in the kitchen. He was wearing only his underwear. I froze for a second. Then I slowly backed away. I hoped the man in his tighty-whities didn't see me as I made my way down his driveway. I imagined that he wanted to talk to me about as much as I wanted to talk to him in that state of dress.

It didn't take long for me to begin to observe how many houses still were displaying their Christmas decorations. Months after the holiday had past, I would take note of wreaths and snowmen and strings of lights. I would be sweating in the heat of an Arkansas spring while knocking on a door covered in festive wrapping paper. As I walked between houses, I did the math and estimated that 15 percent of homes must keep up their holiday decorations year-round. I asked other BNC candidates if they had observed the same thing, but most hadn't. Maybe it's just an Arkansas thing.

I also kept track of how many people told me that they were planning on voting for Congressman Womack in the Republican primary. One gentleman told me that he had to vote for the congressman because they had served together in the military. I shook his hand and thanked him for his service. I couldn't argue with that. Another man said he and Womack had gone to high school together. In total, after knocking on thousands of doors throughout my district, I had a grand total of five people tell me they were Womack supporters. Far more often, people would say to me, "Oh, good. I'm so glad someone is running against him." I heard some version of that response hundreds of times. I'll always remember the sweet little old lady in Fort Smith who said to me through her fence with a thick southern accent, "Oh, honey, I pray that you win."

This experience painted a picture I couldn't ignore. I started entertaining questions that had seemed ridiculous months previous. How could someone who had never received less than 72 percent of the vote be so unpopular? How could all of this hard work not translate into something tangible? What if all of the people I chatted with who sounded so dissatisfied with their current representative actually showed up on Election Day?

Scott and I talked often about how our emotions would ping-pong back and forth. One minute, I would be thinking, *I could actually win this thing.* And then the next minute, I would be overcome with how much of a long shot my campaign really was. The hope and the reality were doing unending battle in my mind, and my feelings were never able to settle for long.

A common question at house parties and other events was whether I could actually win. Whenever it was asked, I sensed that the voter wasn't being sarcastic or dismissive. They were looking for a reason to believe that their support would matter. When I answered, I would always be both honest and hopeful.

"It's a long shot," I would say, "but stranger things have happened, right? Did any of us expect Trump to win?"

Everyone wants to vote for an honest politician, even if they suspect that the phrase might be some kind of oxymoron. Voters want someone who will talk straight with them, express a genuine empathy, and be a real person. Without fail, during presidential elections, we're subjected to stories about which candidate a majority of voters would want to join for a beer. We crave relatability and authenticity in our leaders.

Authenticity is very important to me. When we started Vintage Fellowship, we were committed to creating an authentic community. I had read *Good to Great* by Jim Collins, in which he talks about how great organizations figure out the one thing they can do better than any other organization and focus on that. I knew we'd never be the biggest church. We'd never have the best facilities or programs or preaching. We couldn't do any of those things better than all other churches. *But,* I thought, *we could be the most authentic church in the world.* From the very beginning, we set out to be a place where everyone could actually be their true selves. I hoped my authenticity would set me apart as a candidate as well, even when that would inevitably result in some tense conversations.

Not long after the rally of white supremacists in Charlottesville, Virginia, turned deadly, Vanessa, Matt, and I were campaigning in Bentonville, where the public square is dominated by a monument to Confederate soldiers. One voter with a long beard and dark sunglasses asked me if I thought the monument should be removed. Not wanting to judge him by his appearance, I turned the question around, asking him what he thought, hoping to begin a conversation. He supported the monument and asked again my opinion. I told him honestly that it seems to me that these stories are better told in museums than celebrated in public squares. Getting agitated, he replied that people should be free to wear the Confederate flag on their shirts if they want.

"Wearing a shirt is one thing," I replied, "but public property is completely different."

The conversation winded down when I suggested that no matter one's perspective, I thought we all could agree that mowing people down with vehicles, as happened in Charlottesville, was not the way to solve our differences. Thankfully, he agreed.

Far too often, politics is about crafting an image and controlling the narrative. Politicians obsess about photo ops and looking good in the eyes of the voters. They'll only hold town halls with friendly audiences and vet the questions before they're asked. They want to be in command and have all the answers. I'm sure some candidates do this because of their own internal need to be liked, while others think they need to be all things to all people.

Ultimately, though, voters have the power. If we embraced those who are honest—not just about what they believe, but who they really are—if we encouraged leaders to share their doubts and fears, if we voted en masse for truly authentic leaders, how might our country and our culture be reshaped for the better?

The health of our democracy depends on having leaders who are willing to be honest about their positions on the issues, even if it means having to agree to disagree at times. I wonder, however, if our democracy would also be well served by leaders who are willing to admit what is honestly going on in their personal lives and in their hearts and minds. I wonder what impact it would have made if I had found a way to talk more freely about how hard it was to campaign, the toll it was taking on my family, and how scared I was most of the time. Would radical authenticity from a politician turn people off or be more compelling? Would people vote for a truly honest candidate? I'm not sure I ever found the balance with which I felt comfortable enough to give them that choice.

11
Blood on My Hands

★ ★ ★

From Silent to Strident
on the Issue of Gun Violence

Throughout my campaign I didn't shy away from any questions. I answered them all, on everything from abortion to Confederate monuments, honestly and forthrightly, even if I knew the person asking the question didn't agree with me. But one big issue I did not want to talk about on the campaign trail was guns.

Advocates of the Second Amendment are passionate and vocal. They believe that their constitutional, and even God-given, rights are at risk, and many of them have become single-issue voters. Likewise, those who campaign for gun control do so eloquently, quoting statistics and moving stories to make their case. I feared that if someone from either group asked me about my position, I would struggle to answer.

As Scott and I drove up and down the highways of my district going to events, we would discuss various ways to answer the inevitable questions about guns. I couldn't settle on an answer that felt true to me. I knew that when I was asked about it, I stammered and stuttered rather than speaking with confidence and from my heart. At every house party and during every media interview, I silently prayed that the question wouldn't arise. But it often did. I never felt good about what I said.

My struggle was that I wasn't a gun owner and have never been one. I've shot guns a few times with friends, but I've never been hunting and have never felt the need to have a gun in my home to protect my family. Guns just haven't been a part of my experience. I knew this put me out of step with my fellow Arkansans, where nearly 60 percent of people own guns. Arkansas has the second-highest gun ownership rates in the entire country, after Alaska. I didn't want to talk about something about which I was deeply aware of my own ignorance.

That being said, I've never been comfortable in the anti-gun crowd either. Many of my progressive friends have for years crusaded for stricter gun control laws, even to the point of calling for completely disarming the American public. While I was sympathetic to the stories of gun violence I would hear, the truth was that I had never personally experienced gun violence in my own family or circle of friends. I failed to be as sympathetic as I should have been, and so their arguments just didn't resonate with me at all.

I felt like I didn't fit in either one of the very polarized camps. I wasn't a gun owner or an NRA member. Neither was I a gun control advocate. Bottom line: I simply didn't want to talk about it. As long as I didn't have an answer that felt authentic and real, my preference was to ignore the gun issue and hope it went away.

Of course, there was no way that could happen.

Throughout 2017 and 2018, incidents of gun violence continued to rise. The media paid more and more attention to them, and they couldn't be ignored, especially by someone who was running for office. The increasing number of high-profile tragedies made me reflect back on previous incidents.

I remembered the shooting at Columbine High School in the spring of 1999. Twelve students and one teacher were killed that Tuesday. I remember watching the news in horror. I was a youth pastor outside of Boston at the time, and the next night, when the teens in our church gathered for youth group, I led them in a time of discussion and processing. I remember how many of them expressed fear and outrage, but the prevailing mood that night was that this was probably a onetime tragedy. We had no idea it would become a pattern that would continue for a couple of decades.

I also thought back to the day of the shooting at Sandy Hook Elementary School in 2012, when a gunman murdered twenty-six people, including twenty children. Charleigh was in second grade at the time. I distinctly remember watching from our dining room window as she came up the driveway after walking home from school. When she came through the door, I hugged her for a long time. She didn't really know why, but I was just so happy that she was home safe and sound.

I wish these incidents and the countless others like them would have woken me up to the necessity of adequately addressing gun violence, but they didn't. I continued in my ignorance and obliviousness, even into my congressional campaign.

And then the shooting at Stoneman Douglas High School in Parkland, Florida, happened on Valentine's Day 2018. Seventeen people were killed that day, and I could no longer ignore it. Gun violence wasn't going away.

Maybe it was the way the surviving students so openly processed their pain and anger. Maybe it was the way they earnestly argued for reforms that sounded both commonsensical and long overdue. Maybe it was the way they didn't just talk about the issue, but they organized and got other teenagers and adults to mobilize. It felt like something shifted in the country in the wake of the Parkland shooting. I know something shifted in me. Those surviving students were leading, and I was determined to follow.

This student leadership didn't just happen at a distance—on my television screen or computer monitor. It happened at my dining room table too. Calvin, who was a junior at the time, processed with Vanessa and me the trauma he felt. He was angry with adults who couldn't be counted on to take action about gun violence. He felt powerless, forced to go to a school that he wasn't sure was safe. He felt ignored by elected leaders who seemed to dismiss the voices of young people. He was infuriated with politicians who cared more about campaign donations from gun lobbyists than the lives of students. As I listened to him talk, I knew he was right.

My ignorance and indifference were part of the problem. I was one of those adults with whom these young people had every right to be angry. My nonanswers about guns weren't doing anything good for anybody.

That night, I posted on social media that we needed to start politicizing gun violence. For too long, in the wake of an incident of gun violence, politicians have tried to forestall the momentum for reform by saying that it would be wrong to politicize tragedy. They offer their "thoughts and prayers" for the families of victims, but I imagine they really hope the news cycle will change as quickly as possible so that people move on. I wasn't going to move on.

The next day, I took the morning to collect my thoughts and do what I should have done months, if not years, earlier. I started by reading the actual text of the Second Amendment, which says, "A well-regulated Militia, being necessary to the security of a free State, the right of the people to keep and bear Arms, shall not be infringed."

For more than two decades, I have read the text of Bible verses and crafted sermons based on them. The first principle of Bible study I learned back in Bible college was observation—start by simply observing what the text actually says. When I read the Second Amendment this way, I noticed something for the first time. It begins with the phrase "well-regulated." This seemed very significant to me.

Most gun rights activists I know resist the idea of regulation when it comes to firearms. They don't want regulation of any kind about what guns can be purchased, where they can be purchased, or even by whom they can be purchased. They point to the Second Amendment to make their case, but the text itself says that regulation, qualified even with the word "well," is firmly within the parameters of Congress.

Often in politics, we're given false dichotomies—choices

that don't really exist. For instance, we're told that we have to choose between the environment and the economy, but I don't think that's so. Likewise, I don't think we have to choose between commonsense gun reforms and preserving people's right to own guns. The Second Amendment itself holds up both Congress's responsibility to regulate and citizens' rights to bear arms.

Almost like I was preparing a sermon, I reflexively took out a piece of paper and pen and began writing my position on guns. It would no longer be acceptable, either to the public or to me personally, for me not to have a clear and definitive answer on this crucial issue, and the text of the Second Amendment would be my inspiration.

I wrote six actions that I believe our elected leaders in Congress need to take to curb the epidemic of gun violence, especially mass shootings in our schools. Before the day was over, I had published it on social media and e-mailed it to my database of supporters. It was inexcusable that I was part of the problem previously, but I was determined to campaign differently every day after Parkland. I began by saying,

> Parents all over America are wondering if it's safe to send their children to school today. They want a society in which our kids can go to class or the movies without having to worry that they will be gunned down. As a country, we have endured senseless tragedy after senseless tragedy. And in response, our elected officials offer their thoughts and prayers but not their actions. They can't risk upsetting their special-interest donors by doing what the vast majority of Americans expect them to do—take the steps necessary to build a safer society.

Reminding voters that I was not receiving money from any corporate donors or special-interest groups, and therefore could speak honestly and forthrightly about what needs to be done to address the plague of school shootings and gun violence in America, I laid out my plan to meaningfully address gun violence in America.

Commonsense Gun Laws

The vast majority of Americans are unified in their belief that we can preserve our Second Amendment rights while also enacting commonsense gun laws. Congress needs to act immediately in banning automatic and semiautomatic weapons, closing loopholes that allow guns to be purchased at shows and online, banning bump stocks, and establishing a national permit-to-purchase program that includes effective background checks. None of these reforms infringe on any law-abiding citizen's ability to own a gun, but they do reduce the likelihood that the wrong types of weapons get into the hands of the wrong kinds of people.

Comprehensive Threat Assessment in Every School in America

Experts agree that when schools conduct a comprehensive threat assessment, they are better prepared to identify and respond to potentially tragic situations. The Department of Education needs to create a template for a comprehensive threat assessment that must be conducted in every school in America before the beginning of the next school year. Ensuring the safety of our children needs to be the singular top priority of every school board in America, and through the Department of Education, they need to have the resources necessary to make student safety the top priority.

Study the Links between Gun Violence, Mental Illness, and Adolescent Medication

Whenever a mass shooting takes place in America, much of the ensuing conversation revolves around whether the shooter was mentally ill. Often this discussion is used to deflect attention from other needed action, like commonsense gun law reform. However, it is incumbent upon us to establish clearly whether there is a link between mental illness and mass shootings or between school shootings and adolescent use of certain medications. The president needs to establish an independent blue-ribbon commission to conduct this study, and then Congress needs to implement its recommendations.

Explore Liability Insurance for Gun Owners

The law requires citizens in almost every state to purchase insurance when they become owners of motor vehicles. When people have such insurance, they are incentivized by insurance companies to get lower rates in exchange for freely choosing to enact certain behaviors, such as maintaining a perfect driving record. If gun owners were required to purchase liability insurance, they too would have a financial incentive to enact greater safety procedures in their homes, thus reducing the risk of accidental and intentional gun violence.

National Dialog about the Myth of Redemptive Violence

We need a national conversation about what we believe about violence. For too long, we've glorified violence in our entertainment and have told ourselves formative narratives that reinforce the myth of redemptive violence, which is that the only way to overcome violence is through greater, more overwhelming violence. Unfortunately, our politicians often reinforce this narrative in their rhetoric. From kitchen tables to boardrooms, from classrooms to legislative chambers, we need to talk realistically and honestly about the role we want violence to play in our society. Perhaps an Ad Council campaign that seeks to reframe the conversation can enhance this dialog, as has been successful with texting and driving, recycling, and other issues.

Campaign Finance Reform

Ultimately, every issue in the current American political climate is a financial one. Our elected officials can't be trusted to put the needs of people first because they are beholden to the corporations and special-interest groups that fund their campaigns. We won't have leadership willing to take these necessary steps until we elect leaders who do not take money from the gun industry, the pharmaceutical industry, and their lobbyists.

The reaction to my plan was predictable. Gun enthusiasts sent me hateful messages on social media. I got into an argument with a couple of guys at the cigar lounge I frequent. I knew I was giving Congressman Womack something he could use to criticize me with his conservative base. The positive reaction, however, was even more overwhelming. I received personal notes of thanks from gun control advocates who easily could have dismissed me as being late to the game. The day I sent the e-mail, I had my single best day of fund-raising for the whole campaign. People were looking for tangible steps, and I was finally offering them.

I went on to receive the Moms Demand Action Candidate of Distinction recognition, the first candidate in my race—Republican or Democrat—to do so. I attended several Moms Demand Action gatherings and won the support of their leadership.

More than the external reaction, though, I felt a weight lift emotionally. I had been carrying around the burden of what I knew was an inadequate response to an important issue. I now knew I could answer questions on principle and with confidence.

A few weeks after the Parkland tragedy, students in my district organized a March for Our Lives rally in Bentonville. I decided to spend the morning canvassing near the park where the rally would be held before meeting up with Calvin to attend.

I went up and down several streets that morning, knocking

on doors and introducing myself to voters. But there was one house I skipped. It was at the end of a long street and had yard signs for both President Trump and a woman who was running for governor of Arkansas. She was the owner of a shooting range and organized her whole campaign around protecting gun rights. I knew it would be a waste of time to stop by that house.

As I made way down the street, I noticed that a man and woman had emerged from the house that I skipped. He was wearing a bright-red Make America Great Again hat, and she had on a T-shirt that espoused her very conservative views. They saw me going door to door and waited for me at the end of a driveway.

"What are you up to?" the man called to me.

I knew I couldn't avoid them. "I'm Robb Ryerse, and I'm running for Congress. I'm challenging Steve Womack in the Republican primary."

"We're not big fans of that guy. He's too much of an establishment politician," he replied.

I agreed with him and tried to steer the conversation toward how we need representatives who will put the needs of people ahead of corporate donors. They expressed some affinity but started asking me about specific issues. Their faces dropped when I told them I supported Medicare for All and some other progressive issues.

"Are you sure you're a Republican?" she asked.

I chuckled at the all-too-familiar question and assured them I was. I gave them one of my cards and told them to check out my website.

Before I broke away to continue my door-knocking, the man wearing the MAGA hat said, "We're headed down to the park to see this rally those silly kids have organized."

I took a deep breath and said, "Yeah, I'm going too, but I'm going to be standing with those students and the folks who want commonsense gun reforms."

They just walked away, and I knew I wouldn't be getting their votes.

When I got to the rally, I found Calvin among the hundreds of people who were gathering. He was carrying a sign that he had made. It read, "You have blood on your hands." Next to those words were pictures of Senator Tom Cotton and Representative Steve Womack. My stomach sank.

"Man, I can't have my picture taken with you carrying that sign," I told him. "It's just a little too controversial for the campaign." But I knew he was right. Any politician who refused to take action on needed gun reform did have blood on their hands. Maybe I did too.

We listened and cheered as students told their stories and spoke passionately and eloquently about the trauma of growing up in an era of gun violence. I made mental notes about points that I could echo during the campaign. I let them inspire and motivate me. These students were leading the nation, and they were leading me.

12

The Only "NeverTrumper" in the Room

★ ★ ★

Insiders, Outsiders, and the Trouble with Tribalism

One of the mistakes grassroots candidates make is spending more time at events hosted by their political party than at the things that will bring them face-to-face with actual voters. The allure of getting party support is strong, and it's understandable that candidates would want the party bigwigs to notice them. But of far greater importance is investing time, energy, and resources in activities like house parties and door-knocking.

As a progressive Republican, I was confident that my stances on the issues would have a better audience with rank-and-file voters than with GOP bosses anyway. Polls show that the majority of Republican voters support Medicare for All, ending the practice of family separation at the border, and increasing the top marginal tax rate, for instance. Yet very few elected Republican leaders are willing to advocate for the things that are popular with voters. Party leadership is out of step with its own constituency, which I believe will pose a significant problem in the future for conservative Republicans who currently dominate the establishment.

Because of this, I committed early on that I would not waste my time trying to court Arkansas Republican leadership but would take my campaign directly to voters. I simply wasn't going to fill up my calendar driving all over my district going to every Republican Party event hosted by a local county chapter. I was sure it would be both personally frustrating and a waste of time. However, if I was invited by a group to come to their event, I decided that I would attend.

One such invitation arrived in the mail. The Marion County Republican Party was hosting its annual Reagan Day Dinner about six weeks before the primary and asked me to be there. I responded that I would, and Vanessa and I put it on our calendars.

Marion County is at the far edge of my district. It is a rural county in the Ozark Mountains. It is home to towns with names like Yellville and Flippin. The folks who live there are farmers and factory workers. Their homes are very spread out, making door-to-door canvassing difficult. The total population of Marion County is just a fraction of the city where I live. So, I knew I wouldn't spend much time in this part of the district during the campaign, but I wanted to make sure I got out there. The Marion County Republican Reagan Day Dinner seemed like the perfect opportunity.

Congressman Womack was also scheduled to attend, which got Josh and the documentary film crew very excited. Up to this point, they hadn't been able to capture footage of Congressman Womack, and they thought having both of us in the same room would make for a dramatic scene. Josh reached out to the chair of the Marion County GOP to get permission to film the dinner. The prospect of having a camera crew from New York City descend on their event made them nervous, but Josh was able to develop a good rapport with the chair, who, coincidentally, had moved from the bustle of Long Island to the seclusion of rural Arkansas many years earlier. They got the clearance they needed.

As the day drew closer, I became more anxious about it. I simply didn't know what to expect. My mind raced with questions. *How would I be received? Would I have opportunity to talk to the group? If so, would I mention progressive policy or speak more about my role as an antiestablishment candidate, hoping to appeal to an audience that I knew voted overwhelmingly for*

President Trump? What would I say to Congressman Womack if we were to meet again?

In my mind, I pictured the event being a lot like the countless church potlucks I have attended throughout the years. Before moving to Arkansas, I pastored a church in rural Michigan. I imagined myself eating Jell-O salad off of a paper plate while trying to make small talk with senior citizens. Only this time, there would be a cameraman filming it.

About a week before the dinner, Congressman Womack cancelled. He was needed in Washington and wouldn't be able to attend. Josh was devastated; I was relieved. At least one potentially uncomfortable conversation had been averted.

Vanessa and I discussed what I should wear. What does one wear to the Marion County Republican Reagan Day Dinner? The flier mentioned cowboy hats and boots. Vanessa laughed uncontrollably at the thought of me donning either. Few things would be more out of character for me. I remembered my commitment to never pander for votes, and I decided to wear jeans and a blazer, along with my regular Sperry loafers.

The day of the dinner was actually a very busy one for me. Charleigh and I attended the March for Science in Fayetteville first thing in the morning. This felt like much more my crowd, and as we marched I happily talked to voters about how important it is that we take climate change seriously.

When the March for Science ended, I dropped Charleigh off at home and sped to a forum about immigration issues being hosted by local Latinx activists. The forum was organized for candidates for office to hear directly from Hispanic and Marshallese members of our community about their stories and experiences. I arrived late and joined Vanessa, who had saved me a seat. We learned a lot during the forum. I was sorry I had to leave early, but before I did, I was proud to sign a pledge that I would have campaign literature in Spanish, have a Spanish version of my website, and intentionally campaign in the Hispanic areas of my district. Thanks to the hard work of my volunteers, I was the first candidate to sign the pledge who actually delivered on every single promise I made. On my way out of the forum, I was waylaid by the Spanish-language television station in our area, which wanted to interview me.

By this point, I was running late to meet up in Rogers with a dozen of my volunteers who had spent the day knocking on doors for me. The temperature that day was colder than usual, and everyone had pink cheeks when we gathered in a park. They had been at it for hours, and I didn't want to keep them any longer, but I did want them to know how deeply grateful I was that they would devote a Saturday to helping me.

After seeing them off, I rushed home to get changed so that Vanessa and I, camera crew in tow, could make the two-hour drive to Summit, where the dinner was being held. We chatted nervously as we drove, stopping occasionally to jump out and put up a few campaign signs in areas we hadn't reached yet.

We drove up to the Marion County Fairgrounds and parked in a field with dozens of other cars. The documentary crew put microphones on Vanessa and me. We took each other's hand. There was no backing out of this now. Outside of the building was a Ronald Reagan lookalike on a horse. People were getting their pictures taken with him. We decided not to.

Inside, the room was crowded with long tables and chairs. People were milling around the edges. I counted how many Make America Great Again hats there were compared to cowboy hats. I was glad to be wearing neither. One rather exuberant young man was wearing an American flag suit. The woman at the registration table had on a large brooch that spelled out "TRUMP." I whispered to Vanessa that we should get a cup of coffee. I doubted they had anything stronger.

I don't enjoy small talk, especially with strangers, which I realize is not ideal for a politician. I took some deep breaths and told myself that having a panic attack at this moment would probably be the worst thing possible for my campaign. I was there to glad-hand with voters, so I needed to get on with it.

In the corner of the room, I began a conversation with a young man. His fiancé was running for county treasurer. When I told him that I was challenging Steve Womack in the primary, he replied that he'd probably vote for me. "I always vote against incumbents if I can," he said. "I don't like career politicians and think we should throw the bums out." I thought to myself that if there were enough antiestablishment voters like him in the rural counties, we might just have a chance to win.

I bumped into a man who was running for Arkansas Supreme Court. I recognized him from his campaign commercials, which made it clear that he was a Trump Republican. We chatted for a bit, and when I told him about my race, he replied, "Oh! You're taking on a big fish." I couldn't tell if he was saying it with admiration or derision.

Everyone seemed to know each other. Either they were Marion County Republican regulars or they were well-known establishment politicians. It seemed like conversations were easy for everyone except us. Vanessa and I tried to work the room, but every conversation was made exponentially more awkward by the cameraperson standing just a few inches away. Throughout the night, I had a sound technician holding a boom mic overhead, recording every word. The crew had been following me around for months, and I had become accustomed to them. But no wonder the folks of Marion County were hesitant to engage.

After what felt like an eternity, I decided to head to the bathroom to catch my breath. I stepped up to a urinal and realized that standing next to me was the state chairman of the GOP. We had met in Little Rock right before I paid my exorbitant fifteen-thousand-dollar filing fee. We didn't exchange words until we were washing our hands. I asked him his thoughts about whether the predicted "blue wave" in the midterm elections would reach Arkansas. Unsurprisingly, he was dismissive. I was just glad that I had thought of some way to engage him.

When I found Vanessa again, I told her that we needed to introduce ourselves to the governor and the lieutenant governor. We waited our turn to talk to Governor Asa Hutchinson. When I told him who I was and that I was running against

Steve Womack, he seemed to have a look of recognition wash over his face. He immediately begged out of the conversation and moved on from us. I whispered to Vanessa, "There is no way he wants his picture taken with me."

As I approached the lieutenant governor, Tim Griffin, I decided I would mention to him that we had a mutual friend. One of the people who had once worked on one of his campaigns had also attended Vintage Fellowship a few times. However, in my nervousness, after I introduced myself, I embarrassingly botched my friend's name. I don't know why I did it, but I just drew a blank. The lieutenant governor had no idea who I was talking about. That conversation ended as painfully as any other that night.

Vanessa and I decided to make our way to one of the tables and see if we could get into a longer, more authentic conversation with someone before dinner was served. We sat down by a couple who looked to be about our age. We learned that she was running for reelection as county judge. As we talked about family and kids, I noticed that she was wearing more makeup than I had ever seen on a woman. Under her cheekbones, her face was painted bright white. *No matter how hard we tried*, I thought, *it's like we are unable to escape the bizarre.*

Mercifully, a bluegrass band took the stage and drowned out the chatter in the room. When they were done, a prayer was offered, and dinner was served. During the meal, a variety of speakers were invited to the stage. I was not one of them. The governor lauded his work bringing technology jobs to the state, but I was pretty confident Marion County hadn't reaped the benefits of that. The lieutenant governor was the keynote speaker, and he began by saying that he had just been texting with Congressman Womack. I wondered if they were texting about me. "The congressman is busy working for you in Washington, DC, tonight and sends his regrets that he can't be here," he said.

When the speakers were done, the emcee, a state senator, began introducing all of the candidates who were present at the dinner.

"We want to welcome my good friend, Governor Asa Hutchinson."

Everyone applauded.

"We want to welcome my good friend, Lieutenant Governor Tim Griffin."

Everyone applauded.

On down the list he went, introducing each and every elected official or candidate with the same qualifier, "my good friend." Until he got to me.

"We want to welcome . . . uh . . . Robb . . . Rears. . . . I'm sorry. I don't know how to pronounce it." No one ever does. I tried to say "Rye-Er-See" loudly enough for him to hear, but he didn't. I stood up and gave a little wave.

Everyone applauded, but even my introduction had turned out to be awkward.

When dinner and the program were over, Vanessa and I headed for the door. There was no good reason to stick around and continue to make cumbersome conversation. The documentary crew met us in the field-turned-parking-lot and took off our mics. We got in the car, and before I started it, I said to Vanessa, "I don't ever want to do that again."

"Me either," she replied.

We drove home mostly in silence. Every once in a while, one of us would say, "That was awful," and we would laugh. And then we would be quiet again.

I look back on the Marion County Republican Party Reagan Day Dinner as one of the worst events of my campaign. An evening of making small talk with strangers is always going to be difficult for me, but the alienation I felt was my lasting impression. I'm a pastor, but the prayer offered before dinner that included partisan loyalty to the president made me cringe. I'm a Republican, but the vapid criticism of Democrats sounded juvenile to me. I'm a politician, but the speeches given by elected leaders rang hollow with their lack of substance. I instinctively knew that the only people in the room who hadn't voted for President Trump were me, Vanessa, and probably the four members of the documentary crew—and if anyone else knew that, we wouldn't be welcome.

Feeling like an outsider in a group of people is a difficult thing. In one respect, given our shared party affiliation, this should have been my tribe. We should have had some common ground from which to build a connection. Yet I could not relax enough to be myself. Welcoming a newcomer didn't seem important to the people at the dinner, and I was unable to overcome the barriers.

That dinner stood in sharp contrast to the other events of the day.

I'm pretty confident that there weren't many Republicans at the March for Science I had attended in the morning. Nonetheless, I was able to easily talk with people, including Democrats who were running for local office. Several people went out of their way to come over and say they were glad I was there. We shared a concern that science, especially climate science, needs to be taken more seriously in our national dialog. The atmosphere was inclusive, a space where conversations could take place.

The immigration forum Vanessa and I attended that day was designed to inform and educate candidates for office. The audience included Democrats, Republicans, and Libertarians, and the organizers had a definite agenda. They advocated for policies that not everyone in the room agreed with, but they made their case respectfully and compellingly. They didn't demonize those who might disagree with them, but instead shared personal stories of how our current immigration system had made their lives more difficult. For anyone listening with an open mind, those stories were hard to dismiss. Uniformity didn't appear to be their goal, but broadening people's perspectives was. They accomplished that goal with both conviction and grace.

Too often, political spaces in our society, whether online or in person, are dominated by partisanship and tribalism. They foster exclusion, forcing people to take sides. They result in an

atmosphere of us-versus-them. They stifle questions and reinforce blind loyalty.

It is becoming harder to create a space where people from
different tribes and perspectives can come together. Pro-life
Democrats, evangelicals in the midst of theological deconstruc-
tion that puts them at odds with their church, even privileged
allies for minority groups often feel alone when they don't pass
a litmus or purity test established by the groups to which they
belong. Leaders of these groups need to realize that it takes a
willingness to listen, not just preach. Recognition that people
are at different places in their personal journey is required. So
are respect and inclusion. Politics needs to be about more than
just winning; it needs to be about how we connect with one
another for the common good, even when we come from different points of view and parties.

The grand experiment of my campaign was to attempt to
transcend these divisions. I wanted to give people an alternative, where the letter after my name on the ballot was not the
most important thing. While I spoke boldly about the issues I
believe in, I also tried to make the underlying point that even
agreeing on policy is not the most important thing. For me, the
fundamental presupposition of politics is that we must elect
leaders who will put the needs of people first. I wholeheartedly
believe that all people need someone who will represent them
in all levels of government.

At the end of that long and difficult day, I hadn't felt welcomed by members of my own party. I felt more at home
with climate and immigration advocates because they warmly
invited me in. They shared their stories, their passions, and
their lives with me. They were more concerned about people
learning, growing, and developing than agreeing. I wanted my
campaign to be more reflective of that kind of openness and
receptivity than the exclusivity of partisanship. I believe I was
better for it, and the country would be as well.

13

Why Do You Vote
the Way You Do?

★ ★ ★

Personal Interest or the Common Good

The closer we got to Election Day, the greater my sense was that our long-shot campaign was a far bigger long shot than we had ever imagined. The fleeting feelings of "we could win this thing" came with much less frequency. I had endeavored to do something that hadn't been done before, namely provide Congressman Womack with a primary challenge. I had campaigned hard, but in the closing days I began to talk to Scott about the math of the election.

"We absolutely have to win Washington County," I told him. "But even if we do, if we lose Benton County, there's no way we can win. And that doesn't even take Fort Smith, Russellville, or any of the rural counties into consideration. It just looks bleak to me."

All Scott could do was concur and encourage me to keep knocking on doors so that I could talk to as many voters as possible.

A ray of hope came a couple weeks before Primary Day when the editor in chief of the *Arkansas Democrat-Gazette* called. Their editorial board was going to endorse someone in my race, and they wanted to talk to me before they made their decision. I thought that an endorsement from the only major newspaper in the district could make a huge difference.

On the morning of my meeting with the editorial board,

Scott and I drove to their offices. We lingered in the waiting room, discussing how even though the building was very large, we could only see a few employees working in cubicles. We talked about how the media landscape had changed, and newspapers might very well be an endangered species. Nonetheless, the newspaper wasn't going to go away before my primary, and I needed to do my best to get their endorsement, even if its impact wouldn't be what it might have been a decade earlier.

When we were taken to the room for our meeting, I realized that I knew one of the members of the editorial board. She had been with the paper a long time and used to write articles for the religion section. When we had started Vintage Fellowship, she had done a very nice write-up about the church. She also had covered the publication of my first book, penning a positive profile about me. Seeing her again gave me some encouragement that I might have an ally on an editorial board that I was sure would be skeptical of my campaign.

They were indeed skeptical. They asked all of the typical questions, the ones I had been asked hundreds of times already. They wanted to know my stand on abortion, on gun control, on taxes, and on all the usual issues. By this point, I was confident and stuck to my well-worn answers. Message discipline was working in my favor once again. But their skepticism became evident when they asked about how aligned I was with the Republican voters of Arkansas's Third Congressional District. They noted that this was a district that went heavily for President Trump in 2016 and that its voters were known for being quite conservative. They wanted to know if my progressive stand on the issues was representative of the people in our area.

In response, I tried to make the case that the voters of my district were decidedly antiestablishment—that they wanted to "drain the swamp" and didn't trust career politicians like Congressman Womack. I also cited polls that showed Republican voters in surprisingly large numbers actually support progressive policies when asked about them specifically. I told them, as I had told just about anyone who listened to me during the campaign, that I believe the voters of my district deserved a choice in this election, and I was giving them that choice. They also deserved someone who would actually represent them in Washington, and because I wasn't a politician, I'd be able to do that.

"You're not a politician?" asked the editor in chief. "Well, you didn't wear your earring today, and that seems like the kind of calculation a politician would make."

Did he just ask me about my earring? I thought.

I stammered something about how I had just forgotten to put it in that morning and that whether I wore an earring had nothing to do with how well I could represent the people of my district. But I could read the skepticism all over his face. He didn't believe me. I wondered if he doubted everything else I had said during the interview.

When the meeting ended, Scott told me that he thought I had done an excellent job, the best job possible under the circumstances. We agreed that at the very least I hadn't made a fool of myself. We also agreed that an endorsement was probably unlikely, but it would be a game changer if it happened.

A week or so later, I got a Google alert in my e-mail. My name had shown up on a website. It turned out to be the website for the *Arkansas Democrat-Gazette*, which had published their endorsement in my race. I clicked on the link and held my breath.

The editorial board had decided to endorse Congressman Womack.

Their rationale was exactly what Scott and I had expected. Congressman Womack had recently become chair of the Budget Committee in the House of Representatives. He was building his clout within the party, and that, they reasoned, would benefit our district. Besides, they said, my positions were far too progressive for our conservative district.

Not getting their endorsement wasn't what bothered me most, however. They spelled my name wrong in their editorial. They referred to me as "Rob Ryerse," leaving the second "b" off of Robb. I understand, that in the grand scheme of things, this was a very minor slight, but I felt completely disrespected. Their minor infraction gave me something to be angry about that deflected my disappointment about not getting their endorsement. I stewed about it all day, even to the point of writing an e-mail to the editor in chief about how unprofessional it was for them to misspell my name. I ended up not sending the e-mail because I didn't want to seem petty.

If I couldn't count on an endorsement from the newspaper to sway voters, I was left with wondering what actually motivates people to show up on Election Day and to cast their ballots the way they do.

In my mind, one of the lessons of the 2016 presidential election is that a significant number of voters feel disenchanted with the two major political parties and their establishment candidates. Senator Bernie Sanders's meteoric rise from statistical insignificance in the polls to giving Hillary Clinton a run for her money in the Democratic primary typified this unrest. By boldly advocating for big ideas and running as an outsider who depended not on corporate PACs and superdelegates but rather on the support and organization of grassroots activists, Senator Sanders showed that antiestablishment candidates can have great appeal to the electorate. Senator Sanders may have made his case so well that some percentage of his supporters were never going to vote for Hillary Clinton in the general election, which may have unwittingly helped Donald Trump. For some voters, purity is more important than pragmatism.

Donald Trump himself is evidence of the power of antiestablishment voters. In a crowded Republican primary, he was able to carve out a niche of committed supporters who wanted to see what would happen if we elected a businessman rather than a traditional politician to the highest office in the land. His many primary opponents and Hillary Clinton with all of their experience in government were the perfect foils for his drain-the-swamp rhetoric.

I am sympathetic to the antiestablishment motivation for voting, and I hoped it would help me in my primary. However,

I don't think it can be the sole reason why someone votes the way they do. While I agree that we need to replace as many career politicians as possible, I think we need to replace them with people who are accomplished in their chosen fields, who are of high moral character, and who have compelling ideas to fix the biggest problems we face as a country. If a newcomer to politics doesn't have these three characteristics, maybe voting for someone who has spent much of their career in government is the way to go.

A significant percentage of the electorate, especially among conservatives, are single issue voters. I've seen countless "I Vote Pro-Life" bumper stickers, and I know that many people will simply never vote for a candidate who supports a woman's right to bodily autonomy. In presidential elections, these voters cast their ballot for the person they believe will appoint Supreme Court Justices who are "strict constructionists," which is code for antiabortion. No matter how much they need to hold their noses when casting their ballot, for single-issue abortion voters, a candidate claiming to be pro-life covers a multitude of sins. While I believe the abortion issue is much more nuanced than these voters are willing to admit, if you sincerely believe that life begins at conception and that abortion is an American holocaust claiming the lives of millions of unborn babies, it's hard to convince these voters that any other issue is of such great importance.

Another large group of single-issue voters are motivated by their belief that they have a constitutional and divine right to own guns. They've been convinced by gun manufacturers and their powerful lobby that their freedoms are under attack. If they are made to surrender their guns, then all of their other freedoms could be taken away as well. They think that a slippery slope to tyranny awaits us if any concessions on the gun issue are made. The Second Amendment is their Scripture, and they'd never consider voting for someone who wants common-sense gun reform.

In politics, the conventional wisdom is that most people, while not single-issue voters, are motivated primarily by the economy. More specifically, they are motivated by their own economic situation. These voters care most about their own wallet and bank account. In 1992, James Carville famously built Bill Clinton's successful presidential campaign around the mantra of "It's the economy, stupid." In that election, and in just about every one since, politicians have tried to appeal to voters based on how electing them will translate into a stronger economy and better-paying jobs.

Ironically, some voters who are motivated by economic issues tend to vote against their own immediate benefit. They vote not for what will be best for them now, but rather what will be best for them once they achieve their dream of economic success. Many working-class Republican voters have bought into the idea that tax cuts for the rich will have a trickle-down effect that benefits everyone. *Besides, they think, once I become rich, I don't want to give a huge percentage of my income to the government in taxes.* The reality is that very few of these voters are ever going to realize their dreams of profound wealth, but nonetheless, money motivates their electoral decision-making.

In the aftermath of Trump's election, a slew of articles analyzed how he was able to accomplish his unexpected success. Over and over again, it was suggested that "economic insecurity" drove white, rural voters to cast their ballots for Trump. While I believe there is undoubtedly some truth to that, I also think it's equally true that "economic insecurity" was a cover for racist, xenophobic, and misogynistic motivations. Some significant percentage of Trump voters feared that their jobs and even their way of life were put in jeopardy by immigrants and women gaining too much power. The rhetoric of nationalism, America First, and Make America Great Again drew them to the candidate they thought best understood their plight, even if he had no personal experience with what it's like to be a poor, rural American.

There is also no way to discount the role that party loyalty plays in people's voting patterns. Some people simply believe that their party is completely right and the other party is completely wrong. Whether it's the #BlueNoMatterWho voters who were vocal on social media in the 2018 midterms or Republican voters who think Democrats want to turn the United States into a European-style socialist country, the letter after a candidate's name is the deciding factor in the voting booth.

Given the diversity of the American electorate—or even the differences that exist in one area like Arkansas's Third Congressional District—and the myriad motivations that go along with it, any candidate for office can find it difficult to break through the noise and connect with the mental, emotional, and psychological reasons that people vote the way they do. I didn't know if my progressive and antiestablishment message would be able to crack the code and propel me to victory on Election Day. All I could do was stay on message, stay true to myself, and hope that it would.

I have come to believe that we need a new electoral motivation in American politics. Rather than voting based on our own pet issues or our own economic interests or our own party affiliation, I think people ought to vote based on the common good.

Letting the common good motivate our Election Day decisions means voting for the candidates who are advocating for policies that will do the most good and have the greatest positive impact. It means setting our personal interests aside and considering the needs of others. The common good is about what is good for all people, not just me and my family or people who think the way we do. My perceived rights and privileges might actually be subservient to the needs of my neighbors, be they next door, in my town, or on the other side of the country.

The common good should especially be the motivation for Christian voters. In Philippians 2:3–4, the Apostle Paul admonishes Jesus' followers to "Do nothing from selfish ambition or conceit, but in humility regard others as better than yourselves. Let each of you look not to your own interests, but to the interests of others." I can't help but think that the application of this text must expand beyond personal interactions and that the purview of doing nothing out of selfish ambition and personal interest must include voting.

If I vote purely to protect my right to own a gun while ignoring the cries of parents and students traumatized by gun violence, am I doing something out of selfish ambition and personal interest? If I vote for the candidate who promises me the biggest tax cut while ignoring the people whose lives are impacted by cuts to the social safety net, am I doing something out of selfish ambition and personal interest? If I vote because of nationalistic or party loyalty while ignoring those with a different country of origin, am I doing something out of selfish ambition and personal interest? If I vote to preserve a culture in which I am most comfortable while ignoring people who have been marginalized, am I doing something out of selfish ambition and personal interest?

I think it is incumbent upon Christian voters to wrestle with these questions and consider whether their voting patterns have been shaped more by the cultural norms of self-preservation and self-interest than the truly biblical values of humility and sacrifice. I also think Christian leaders in the political space need to call Christian voters to this higher standard instead of feeding their fears and insecurities. Rather than our own interests being of utmost importance to us, we need to be reminded of what Paul says: that as followers of Jesus, the interests of others need to be our motivation.

With this motivation, I would be concerned about people being paid a living wage, even if I have a good job that pays me enough to support my family and save for the future. I would care about undocumented people who are treated unjustly by our immigration system, even if my ancestors once came to America "the right way." I would recognize the crushing reality of student loan debt on young people, even if I paid off my student loans years ago. I would want the civil rights of others to be protected, even if I haven't personally faced discrimination. I would want to address climate change, even if I don't live in a region with an immediate fear of rising sea levels. I would want everyone to have health coverage, even if I have a good insurance plan through my employer. I would be willing to say that "black lives matter," even if I am white. I would work for criminal justice reform, even if I don't have a loved one who is wrongfully incarcerated.

Another way to phrase Paul's exhortation to look out for the interests of others is to do everything for the common good. The common good might mean getting less for me but more for others. If I vote for the common good, I may have to wait for my personal pet issue to be addressed while the issues others are raising take center stage. I may have to pay a little more in taxes so that needed services can be extended effectively to others. I may have to accept having less influence in the system than I had exercised before so that those whose voices have been marginalized can be better heard. The point of the common good is that I refuse to take the seat of prominence so that it can be given to someone else.

White Christians in America especially need this renewed perspective. White evangelicals and white mainliners have enjoyed decades, if not centuries, of privilege in our country. We have not faced persecution or been marginalized. Rather, we have exercised an outsized amount of influence on American culture. To be a white, straight Christian in America is to have leaders pander to my interests. Instead of demanding that black or brown people or the LGBTQIA community conform to what we want, it is time for us to recognize how our privilege has made life more difficult for others, how we've been overwhelmingly selfish and ambitious, and how out of sync we've been with our expressed values. White Christians in America need to repent and then begin to vote accordingly.

Jesus said that the greatest commandment is to love God and others as we love ourselves. This is not two commandments, but one, a unified vision of love. It is recognizing that when we love others, we love God. When we feed the hungry, visit the incarcerated, welcome the stranger, and care for the sick, we are serving not just other people but Jesus himself. These actions represent humility and sacrifice in action for the common good. Further, love is not just expressed in personal or church-sponsored acts of charity. While it is certainly loving to give money or supplies to a person who is homeless, it is also loving, maybe even more so, to vote for candidates whose policies will make homelessness less prevalent in our society.

In fact, maybe the most loving thing I can do when I enter the voting booth is to cast my ballot not for my own interests but for the common good.

14
Election Day

★ ★ ★

Magic Wands and Mustard Seeds

The Republican primary in Arkansas's Third Congressional District was held on May 22, 2018. It was a day that started like any other in our home. Our kids piled into our room for morning prayers. Throughout the school year, we start our days together, touching base about what we have going on and asking for God's help. We also say the Lord's Prayer together. On Election Day, it wasn't just the kids in our bedroom for prayers. The documentary film crew was there too. Vanessa led us, thanking God for the journey we had been on and asking that no matter how things turned out, we'd have a sense of divine presence and purpose in it all.

We got ready for the day and dropped Charleigh off at school. Election Day fell during the last week of the school year. Calvin had already finished his finals, so he wanted to go with us to the polling place. Vanessa, Calvin, Whimsy, and I drove to the rodeo building in our town, which is where we go to cast our ballots. The documentary crew had permission to film inside, so they followed us.

We took our ballots and walked behind the large touch-screen voting machines. Because it was the only federal race on the ballot, Congressman Womack's and my names were listed first. I hesitated.

My first thought at seeing my name on the ballot was the

immense bizarreness of it all. I thought about myself as a teenager who loved politics and dreamed of running for office but had abandoned that because of my call to be a pastor. What would fifteen-year-old me think of this? Then I thought about the cost of having my name on that ballot. No one in the country had paid as much as I had to be listed as a candidate for office. I expressed again my gratitude for the many people who had helped me pay that fifteen-thousand-dollar fee. Lastly, I thought about the campaign, especially all of the people who had helped and whom I had met along the way. I hoped I had made them both proud and hopeful about the future.

Then I touched the box next to my name. A checkmark appeared. I clicked the "accept" button.

After I finished with all of the other state and local races, I looked down the row of voting booths and saw Vanessa and Whimsy standing in front of another machine. I wondered what Vanessa was thinking. All of this crazy experience had been her idea in the first place. In a very literal way, I could not have done it without her support and encouragement. She had sacrificed so much. I thought about how lucky I was to have a partner like her.

Then I noticed that Tom, the cameraman, had laid his camera on the ground. He wasn't allowed to follow me behind the machine and had been filming from a safe distance. He was fumbling to change something on the camera, maybe the lens or the battery, I didn't know. But I did know that Josh would want the footage of me walking away from the voting booth. I had grown pretty acclimated to how the documentary crew operated, so I stood there and just waited for Tom pick up the camera. It was a long minute or two of just waiting, but when he was ready, I walked away from the voting booth.

I got my "I Voted" sticker from the poll worker and wondered if they had a special batch for candidates that said, "I Voted for Myself." Whimsy came running up to me, followed by Vanessa. Her eyes were red, and tears were on her cheeks.

Outside, Calvin rubbed my back and said he was proud of

me. Then Vanessa and I hugged. We both cried. A mixture of relief and excitement washed over us.

"That was . . . yeah . . . that was a surreal experience," I said to her. I think she felt the same way.

From the rodeo, we headed over to Charleigh's school. They were having an end-of-the-year talent show, and she was going to sing. As we walked into the school gymnasium, a couple of people recognized me and said they had voted for me, which was really encouraging. We stood with some other parents near the bleachers, which were full of students. All of the performers were sitting in chairs on the other side of the gym in order of their performances. Charleigh and I waved to each other.

When her time came, Charleigh walked to the center of the gym and took the microphone. The music for "Landslide" by Fleetwood Mac began to play. Charleigh is a really talented singer and has always delighted us with her voice. Given all that she had been through over the past couple of years, I nearly burst with pride when she started to sing. At the sound of her angelic voice, a cheer went up from the students in the stands. As she headed into the second verse of the song, however, she lost her place and forgot the words. Her head slumped down, and she just stood there. I froze too. I wanted to start singing to help her get back on track, but all I could do was watch. Sensing her embarrassment, the students cheered again to try to reassure her. A couple of her friends ran from the stands to hug her. She made her way back to her chair but didn't stay long. She left the gym, and Vanessa followed her. They stayed in the bathroom for a long time.

If I had a magic wand that would enable me to change only one thing about Election Day, it would be Charleigh's performance at that talent show. Running for office was important, and I wanted to win. But I was a dad before I was a politician. The thing I wanted more than anything was for my daughter to know how proud of her I was. I wanted her to feel self-confidence. I wanted her to know that no matter how she performed, she was loved. I haven't been able to listen to "Landslide" since.

Once we sensed Charleigh was going to make it through the rest of the school day, we headed back to the rodeo. We stood by the side of the road, holding campaign signs, and waving at cars driving by. Each time someone pulled into the rodeo parking lot, I wondered if they would cast their ballot for me. A few folks honked at us as they drove out of the parking lot. Whimsy was three years old at the time, and she quickly grew tired of standing and waving. When she started pulling her dress up over her head and flashing her underwear to voters, we laughed and decided it might be time to wrap it up.

A few hours later, I met Scott and my longtime friend Aaron at our local cigar shop. We smoked good cigars and took stock of the whole campaign. I was deeply appreciative of both their friendship and help during all of it. A leisurely time to reflect with two of my best friends seemed like an apropos way to pass the hours of waiting and wondering until the polls closed.

Throughout the day, I received numerous texts and messages from other Brand New Congress candidates around the country. During our campaigns, we had developed a strong sense of camaraderie. Running a grassroots campaign against the political establishment can be very lonely, and we had learned to be there for one another. We frequently shared best practices with and cheered for each other. We knew what was happening in each other's campaigns. Overall, we had mixed results. Some had won their primaries and some had lost; others still had primary dates upcoming. Nonetheless, we stayed close. My BNC brothers and sisters wished me luck and offered me their support on my big day. On that day in particular, as I had been so often, I was profoundly grateful for them.

That evening, we hosted a watch party at our home. About twenty-five friends showed up to watch election returns with us. We projected a news website with results up on our television and waited for numbers to begin appearing. When the first batch showed up, I had 22 percent of the vote. My heart sank. Even though we had a long way to go until all of the precincts reported, I knew I wasn't going to win.

I whispered to Scott, "I really want to get to 30 percent. Do you think that's possible?"

"I don't know," was all he said.

And then we waited. The website auto-refreshed every ten seconds, but the numbers didn't change. For forty-five minutes we stared at a screen that didn't move. It was excruciating.

When more precincts ended up reporting, my percentage of the vote began to drop. I finished with a little more than 15 percent of the vote. My friends told me how proud of me they were. Some of them even said they were a little surprised I had done as well as I had. I appreciated their kind words, but the results were not what I had worked so hard for. I felt numb.

As it turned out, Congressman Womack ended up spending over $680,000 on the primary campaign against me, a fraction of his reelection war chest. I spent every penny of the $30,000 I had raised. He spent an average of $12 for each vote he received. I spent $1.77 per vote. These numbers proved to me that I had run the kind of race about which I could feel really good. Elections shouldn't be determined by who can raise the most money from corporate PACs and special-interest groups. They should be about who has the best ideas to represent the people of a district. To the very end, that had been my focus and goal. I hadn't pandered. And I hadn't wavered.

Before the watch party broke up, I stood before my assembled friends and thanked them for their help.

"Remember the time we ran for Congress?" I began to laughs and cheers. "That was crazy, wasn't it?"

I went on to tell them that I make a lot of sense about my life out of biblical stories. In the final week of the campaign, I had been thinking a lot about how Jesus used to talk about how change happens. Jesus didn't talk about huge campaigns that blow things away. In the process of bringing about more peace and justice in the world, the things that Jesus talked about were small, insignificant, easily overlooked, 15 percent kind of things.

He often used a metaphor of a seed that would be planted. Small things like seeds can be easily overlooked. People forget about them and don't realize that anything significant is happening below the surface. And then, all of sudden, sometime in the future that thing would sprout and begin to grow. It would bring forth fruit. One of my favorite things Jesus said was that birds from all over would come and make their nests in its branches because it had grown so big and so significant.

When I think about what we attempted to do in Northwest Arkansas and what my Brand New Congress friends all across the country were attempting to do, it was to bring greater peace and justice into the world. That started off as planting a seed. Things didn't go the way we wanted on Election Day, but we planted a seed. Now we had to care for it and tend to it. The political establishment and their corporate donors who are on their way to ruining the country don't have any idea that this seed has been planted. They would look at results of my and other campaigns all across the country and think, "Oh, there's nothing to that." But seeds have been planted that cannot be unplanted.

"So," I told my friends, "I remain really hopeful for the future. I'm really optimistic about what the future holds, not just for us but for our country."

Somebody asked me, "What are you going to do after all of this?"

I said, "The reality is nothing changes. If I win, nothing changes; I'm going to keep trying to serve people and do my best to bring greater justice and peace into the world. And if I lose, that's what we're going to do too."

All of us had voted and worked hard, and we had tried to accomplish something. We didn't get the results we wanted. But the following day and each day thereafter, we can bring justice and peace and love into the world.

I concluded by saying, "I'm a Republican, regardless of what some people might say, and that means that I don't believe we have to have government solutions to all of our problems. Who our representative is is really important, but who our representative is doesn't keep us from bringing love and grace and peace and truth and justice into the world. So that's what we're going to do. We're going to keep working at it, and we're going to keep trying. . . . This is just the beginning of something really good."

Since I was a teenager, I have always had a sense that I was supposed to do something to help change the world. That kind of talk had been commonplace at the youth groups and camps I had attended. It was a familiar refrain in the contemporary Christian music I had listened to. And I absorbed it.

The reason I became a pastor was that I was convinced that the best avenue to change the world was through the work of the church. The reason my path wound back around to politics leading to me running for Congress was that I was dissatisfied with the direction the country was taking under President Trump, and I felt like I needed to do something about it. Complaining about it all to my friends or on social media wasn't enough. I had to get involved.

When we think and talk about changing the world, we often think and talk about what needs to be changed. We focus on the problems and the issues. Then we strategize solutions to those problems. We gin up energy and resources to make it happen. We expect that our passion and excitement are going to carry us on to big things.

What we don't think about very often is how things change. Having a lot of resources and intention in no way guarantees that we're going to be able to bring about change. In fact, change might be far more complicated than we imagine.

Quite frequently, people use the phrase "wholesale change" to describe their attempt to make a big impact in a particular area. Wholesale change is when we try to change everything all at once. Rather than just making a series of minor tweaks to moderately improve things, wholesale change seeks to bring about broad, sweeping, fundamental modifications that will completely overhaul how things are done. Often, however, attempts at wholesale change end up failing because they're too much too soon. Wholesale changes are idealistic, and when they fail, they can leave people feeling disillusioned and discouraged.

When wholesale changes fail, the pendulum typically swings in the other direction, toward embracing the idea of "incremental change." Incremental change is when we try to change things through a slow and steady process. Incremental change creates a step-by-step path that, over a long period of time, will make a difference. Because the movement is slow and deliberate, attempts to bring change incrementally can easily become distracted and derailed. Besides that, to me, the idea of incremental change feels a lot like preserving the status quo for as long as possible.

Near the end of my campaign, I randomly came across a phrase I hadn't heard before, but in my mind, it aptly describes another way that change happens. When I heard this phrase, it captured my imagination. The phrase is "acupunctural interventions." The idea of acupunctural interventions is that small things can make a big difference. Just like the tip of needle can ease a whole lot of discomfort, we can do small things every day that can bring significant and lasting change. This seems to me to be completely in line with the teachings of Jesus. Whether Jesus was talking about faith the size of a mustard seed or how a little bit of yeast makes dough rise or whether he was using a few fish and loaves to feed thousands of people, he celebrated the power of the small.

In the world of politics, it's easy to think that bigger is always better. A campaign's viability is judged almost solely on how much money is raised. More is better. For campaigns that don't take corporate PAC money, small-dollar donations are their life blood. People might think that a donation of a few dollars won't make much difference, but it does. Those donations add up, allowing grassroots candidates like me to get on the ballot, buy needed supplies and advertising, and pay for the tools needed to run a campaign. Until our campaign finance system is revamped, the best—and I believe, only— hope we have for significant and needed change in Washington is working Americans supporting grassroots candidates with the acupunctural interventions of small-dollar donations.

In much the same way, grassroots campaigns are dependent on the generosity of volunteers. What may seem to a person as a small offering of a few hours can make a world of difference to a candidate who doesn't have millions of dollars to hire staffers and paid canvassers. Volunteers who are willing to sacrifice a Saturday to knock on doors or a few hours in an evening to make phone calls to voters have an exponential impact on a campaign.

With the establishment, big-money campaigns getting most of the notoriety and credit, it's easy to see how people often think that their one vote doesn't make much of a difference. They see it as something small and insignificant. The reality couldn't be further from the truth. In elections across the country, and even a few in my own area in 2018, who will represent us was decided by just a few votes. Voting is an acupunctural intervention—something small that makes a big difference.

There are countless opportunities each and every day for us to change the world, in and out of the political season, by being kind, understanding, empathetic, gracious, and generous. It probably won't be big and flashy, but it will be the kind of acupunctural intervention that is desperately needed.

The stump speech I recited hundreds of times during my campaign always started the same way. "My name is Robb Ryerse," I would say, "and I'm the kind of guy who believes in big ideas that are daring enough that they just might happen." That's still true. But my campaign for Congress taught me something else that is equally true. I'm also, now, the kind of guy who believes in small actions that are so impactful that they might just change the world.

15

Lost

★ ★ ★

Learning to Rethink Failure

I woke up the day after Election Day with one main thing on my mind. I had to collect as many of my campaign signs as possible. Arkansas regulations require campaign signs to be picked up within three days of the election. With hundreds of signs dotting the city streets of my district, I knew I had a lot of work to do.

After breakfast, Josh and the documentary crew came to the house one more time. We did a final interview in which Josh asked me how I was feeling about the results. I was honest with him. I was tired and disappointed, but I had an underlying hope that we had started something good. When we finished the recording, they followed me around for an hour or so, filming me pulling signs from the ground and stacking them in the trunk of my car.

After we said our good-byes, I drove a couple of hours to the edge of my district and began working my way back toward home. Whenever we put out a sign, I added the cross streets to a note in my phone. With each sign I retrieved, I deleted the streets from the list. Not every sign was where we had placed it. I wondered if the weather had swept them away somehow or if something more nefarious had happened, like Congressman Womack's staff or supporters had taken them. We'd never really know, and at this point, it wouldn't do me any good to speculate.

It was late when I finally got home. It had rained most of the day, and I was soaking wet and exhausted. But it had been a cathartic day. I had put myself and my name out there for people to judge, and now I was taking my life back, pulling it again within its normal boundaries. I wondered if I was going to be like a rubber band that snapped back to shape after being stretched or if I was going to be more like a sweater that had been stretched out and would never be the same again. Time would tell.

The next day, we packed our luggage and the car and drove to Chicago. Matt had finished their freshman year of college, the other kids had finished school, and we were going on vacation. About a month previously, I had spent a few hours searching online for inexpensive vacations for pastors. I had randomly come across a comment on an old blog that mentioned a house on the Caribbean island of Antigua that pastors could rent for a steep discount. I had e-mailed the owner, and providentially, the week after the election was available.

We flew to Antigua and took a taxi to the house. It sat on a harbor with a deck by the water. We settled in for what we hoped would be a week of much-needed rest and relaxation. It was late when we first arrived, so the next morning, Calvin and I took a golf cart and explored the area. We found a beautiful beach not far from the house where we would undoubtedly spend much of our time. It was Antigua's off-season, so when the whole family returned to the beach a few hours later with our towels and sunscreen, it was like we had the whole ocean to ourselves. We swam and sat in the sun. Admittedly, it was an adjustment not to constantly check my phone or think about if it was time to run off to my next meeting. The water and the warmth helped me transition, emotionally and spiritually.

We spent the next few days having as much fun as we possibly could. Matt, Calvin, and I rode jet skis in the ocean. Vanessa and Charleigh went horseback riding through the mountains of Antigua. We went on an off-road Jeep tour of the island, learning about its history and people, eating its unique cuisine, and seeing beautiful sites. One day, we went snorkeling as a family. Vanessa had brought floaties for Whimsy, and our guide had a small mask she was able to wear. He raved at how well she did, saying that she was the youngest snorkeler he had ever taken out. We saw turtles and fish and even a sunken ship below the water's surface.

When we weren't swimming, we were taking naps or long walks on the beach picking up seashells. The whole week was beautiful.

But eventually we had to return home. The yard signs were all still in the back of my car. There were bills in the mailbox. The grass needed to be mowed. We were returning to real life.

I was going to need to find a job and spent hours sending out résumés and hoping to get called for interviews. We had enough money from Vanessa's big mosaic project to last a little while longer, but eventually I was going to have to go back to work. My friend at the cable company wanted me to return to work for him. I seriously considered it, thinking that maybe I ought to give up trying to change the world and just be content with a "normal" job. I had an offer, but I thought it would be best to wait before making a decision.

In the fall, Calvin would be starting his senior year of high school, so we discussed how it might be good to spend a couple of weeks visiting some of the colleges that were on his short list. We mapped out our trip and decided that to save money we would camp as much as possible, rather than staying in hotels. On a Tuesday morning, we kissed the girls goodbye and headed out on a road trip that would span eleven states and thousands of miles.

We made it to Denver the first day and visited a college. Then we drove north to Wyoming. We were headed to Cheyenne to visit Charlie Hardy. I had met Charlie about a year earlier. At the time, he was promoting a documentary called *Charlie vs. Goliath* about his 2014 run for Congress. Charlie is a former Catholic priest who spent years in Caracas, Venezuela, living among some of the poorest people in the world. He embodies grace and wisdom, and after several phone calls over the course of a year, I treasured his friendship. He was running for office again, this time for the U.S. Senate as a progressive Republican. When we went for a walk after lunch, Charlie told me that my campaign for Congress had inspired him to try again, and I was moved to know that someone with his experience was drawing strength from me.

After a wonderful visit with Charlie, Calvin and I spent the next several days immersed in the unrivaled beauty of the western United States. We camped in the Rocky Mountains. We stopped in Moab, Utah. We toured the unbelievable cliff dwellings at Mesa Verde National Park. We drove across the desert and made it to the Grand Canyon. I had been once before, but it's impossible to tire of its majesty. It's good for my soul to stand beside something so big and feel so small.

Eventually we headed east again, driving across New Mexico and Texas. We spent a couple of days in Austin before making our final stop in New Orleans. As we walked around that historic city, Calvin said, "Dad, thank you. This trip has been amazing." I thought it was too.

Seeing the country, especially parts that I hadn't visited before, reminded me of why it's so important that we continue our work for the good of the country. People aren't just facing problems in Arkansas because they aren't represented well in Washington. The same is happening in many parts of our great nation. In the states we visited, I knew candidates like James Thompson, Stephany Spaulding, Lori Burch, and Adrienne Bell who were running for Congress because they believed like I do that corporate PACs have corrupted our system and things need to change.

When we finally arrived home, I was happy to see Vanessa, Charleigh, and Whimsy again. But I also knew that now, with all of my trips and travels completed, I was going to have to spend some time with myself. I needed the rest and relaxation, the vacation and the distraction. I also needed to do the work of coming to grips with my loss and figure out what was next in my life.

Normally, Vanessa and I see our therapist every six weeks or so. We increase the frequency if there is a particular problem we're trying to solve. In July and August 2018, I was going to see Dr. Freeman every week. We talked about what success and failure really are, whether or not it's worth it to try to make a difference, and what I should do next. I was trying on the idea that I would just get a normal nine-to-five job, spend my evenings watching television, and stop trying to change the world. Our therapist is not the type to offer a lot of answers, but he wasn't buying what I was suggesting. We love him because he listens well, shares theories with us, and sprinkles in enough sarcastic comments that we don't take ourselves too seriously. He just kept repeating to me, "You've done a lot in the past year. It makes sense that you would be tired and wouldn't know what to do next, but you're not going to stop being who you are."

My need to process my defeat leaked out at church too. Each summer at Vintage Fellowship, we observe "Ordinary Time," a recognition that in the church calendar there are not just seasons of celebration but also weeks upon weeks of the ordinary. We use this observance to challenge ourselves to find God in the mundane and regular parts of life, not just in the holidays or crises. Everybody seems to love Ordinary Time at Vintage because our band doesn't play any Christian music. If God can be found everywhere and anywhere, then God can also be found in the music we hear on the radio.

I picked the theme for Ordinary Time that summer based on the lyric from the John Cougar Mellencamp song "Jack and Diane," "Life goes on long after the thrill of living is gone." We sang the song each week, and our worship gatherings explored how God shows up in our everyday disappointments and pain. The thrill of the campaign was gone for me, and I was trying to figure out how my life was going to go on. I think most folks at Vintage knew that I needed this theme more than anybody else, and they were gracious with me about it.

Ultimately, I abandoned my idea of giving up and living a humdrum life of commutes and evening sitcoms. In my heart of hearts, I knew I was just saying I was going to do that because I was afraid of losing again if I tried again to do something big.

The lesson I had to learn, and am still learning, is that daring to do something great and failing is really not failing at all. Certainly, the metrics of success in political campaigns are pretty black-and-white. How many votes did you get compared to your opponent? If you got fewer, you failed, unless, of course, you're running for president and the Electoral College declares you the winner. But that tells only part of the story.

The rest of the story was told by how many people were brought into the process. Before I had even started my campaign, I asked a friend, a former CFO, to run the numbers and figure out if I had a path to victory. Since Congressman Womack had never had a primary challenge, there were no easily comparable races. Using some statistical modeling, he ended up estimating that fifty thousand people were likely to vote in the Republican primary. In the end, fifty-five thousand people voted, and Congressman Womack received fewer votes than he would have expected. I believe that we were able to excite thousands of people about what could be possible if they participated in the process. With a positive, progressive campaign, we were able to grow voter turnout. That certainly wasn't a failure.

Neither was chipping away at the sway the two major political parties have had on our system. I received support from Republicans, Democrats, Libertarians, Green Party members, and independents. I know because they came out of the woodwork to tell me. I ran on a postpartisan message that I would be someone who put people ahead of party, and I asked others to do the same by voting for me. Thousands did. That certainly wasn't a failure, either.

One of the highlights of the campaign for Vanessa and me was getting to fly to Hollywood to be on Rob Bell's podcast. It was hearing about Brand New Congress on the *RobCast* that had originally started this whole adventure. Rob's example and books had been a light for us in the dark days of our faith shift. We were thrilled to spend a few hours in the back house where he records his podcast, sharing our story and soaking in his exuberance. When the podcast aired, it translated into some of our best fund-raising. But more than that, several people in our area heard the podcast and came to visit Vintage Fellowship as a result. Many of them stuck around and have become part of our community. That wasn't a failure.

In the final week of the campaign, one of my friends cornered me on a Sunday morning at church and told me that he had recently received an inheritance and wanted to donate enough money for me to air a television commercial. We hadn't expected that we'd be able to do that and were excited by the possibility. The next morning, Scott filmed me sitting on my porch talking about how the people of Arkansas's Third Congressional District deserved a representative in Washington who would put their needs ahead of corporate donors and lobbyists. We strategized how to make the biggest impact with the commercial, and based on my experience in advertising sales, decided on buying a schedule targeting likely Republican primary voters. In the final days of the campaign, our commercial ran locally and repeatedly on *Fox and Friends* on the Fox News channel. I relished the subversive idea that conservative voters were hearing a progressive message on their favorite news network. That was definitely not a failure.

I demonstrated to my kids that if you see a problem that exists and have the courage to tackle it, it's worth the effort. Cynicism doesn't have to win out. With creativity and hard work, you can try your best to do big things that might just make other people's lives better. My children had front-row seats for a congressional campaign and gained a host of stories they could tell for the rest of their lives. There was no failure in that.

On a personal level, I grew immensely during the campaign. I came to realize that my participation in politics could be a genuine expression of my faith. I could be a Christian involved in politics; one doesn't have to sell one's soul to a corrupt and corrupting system. I spoke truth to that system and found my voice in the process. I went from being a Monday-morning quarterback critiquing and criticizing everything I saw to being on the field, contributing, and moving the ball forward in a way that brought others hope. That certainly wasn't a failure.

Throughout the campaign, I came to understand the role that big money really plays in politics, and I experienced first-hand how difficult the political establishment makes it for regular people to run for office. I now can shed light on a side of the system that most people don't realize. I can tell them my story and the stories of my Brand New Congress slatemates to illustrate how dangerous the establishment finds people who are willing to challenge it. No failure there.

What's more, I gained a host of new friends. From other Brand New Congress candidates around the country to BNC staff and volunteers, from strangers who opened their homes to me to acquaintances who became dear friends, I found my tribe—not among those who share my party affiliation but among the people who are doing what they can every day in big and small ways to make our country a more just and generous place. That certainty wasn't a failure either.

Over and over again during the campaign, I was asked, "Can you really win?" I always answered honestly but somewhat self-deprecatingly, "I don't know, but we're going to find out." Understandably, people didn't want to waste their time or money investing in an effort destined to lose. However, in my campaign and the vision we shared, people found inspiration to participate in ways they never had.

If we only ever invest ourselves in sure things, we'll never develop the courage to overcome our fears and dare to do something great. I may have lost, but I won too.

16

Getting Back on the Campaign Trail

★ ★ ★

We Have a Lot of Work to Do

In August 2018, still unemployed and contemplating a return to advertising sales, I received a phone call from my friend Doug Pagitt that changed my trajectory. He told me that he was starting a new project and wanted to know if I'd be interested in helping. He said it was called Vote Common Good (VCG).

"White evangelicals have been complicit with the Trump administration," Doug explained. "We want to call them to resist their impulse to vote Republican in the upcoming midterm elections and help flip the House to the Democrats."

"That seems like a tall order. How are we going to do that?" I asked.

"We're going to do a bus tour with events in different congressional districts. We're going to use our network of progressively minded pastors to help us host the events. It'll be like an old-fashioned tent revival, but we're calling Christians to repent and vote differently."

That was all I needed to hear. "I'm in," I told Doug.

I became the political director of Vote Common Good. My job on the team was to be the liaison between VCG and the candidates in whose districts we wanted to do events. I had six weeks to coordinate with more than thirty campaigns.

Thankfully, I got some warm introductions from politically connected people who were sympathetic to the work of Vote Common Good, and I started making phone calls and setting up meetings. I was doing a sales job after all, but the product I was peddling was something very unusual.

I had to call candidates or someone from their campaign and sell them on the idea that a group of evangelical pastors and musicians were going to drive into their district, set up a stage and chairs, and run a program that invited religiously minded voters to cast their ballots for those candidates. I knew from my experience as a candidate that we would be a welcome infusion of energy into the campaigns we were going to help. When people think of political campaigns, they often imagine big rallies and giant, cheering crowds. The reality is usually much different—a dozen people in a living room or a few folks sitting around a table at a coffee shop. If we could turn out fifty or a hundred people to an event in a district, it would be among the biggest crowds most congressional candidates would speak to during their campaigns. And we'd do all the work. All the candidates had to do was show up, shake some hands, and share their vision. It was an easy sell.

Those on our burgeoning Vote Common Good team tasked with finding hosts for our events had a much harder sell. We really wanted to host our events in the parking lots of churches, and we found some who welcomed us. But more often, progressive pastors told us no. Many were sympathetic to our cause, but they didn't know if they should mix church and politics, especially if it meant, as some feared, that the appearance of endorsing a candidate as a church could cause them to lose their tax-exempt status with the IRS. Many others were afraid that any Trump-supporting members of their congregations would be upset by our event and didn't want to risk splitting their churches.

As I listened to my VCG teammates express their frustrations about finding locations to host us, I was genuinely conflicted. On the one hand, I understood why pastors would be leery about opening their doors to us. Our idea was new and unproven, and people generally only like to bet on sure things. Even though we explained that using their property for an event was not the equivalent of a candidate endorsement, some just didn't want to take the chance. They also didn't want to open themselves up to criticism. All of it was reasonable. However, a few months before, I had finished a campaign for Congress that came at significant personal cost. Throughout, I was able to navigate the muddy waters of church and politics. At such a critical time for our country, and with the Religious Right continuing to dominate the narrative of how Christians ought to engage in politics, I was deeply frustrated with those progressive pastors around the country who couldn't figure out a way to help us. We pivoted in areas we needed to and found public parks and other venues to hold our events.

We ended up mapping out a cross-country tour that would begin in Pennsylvania and end up in California. In the thirty-six days before Election Day in November, we would hold thirty-one campaign events. Our "band of common do-gooders," as Doug liked to call us, would caravan down the highways of the country with a tour bus, an RV, and a pickup truck pulling our stage. I had never done anything like this—I'm not sure anyone has—but with Vanessa's complete support, I was excited to be getting back into the political game.

The big experiment we were attempting with Vote Common Good is an intriguing one. Eighty-one percent of white evangelicals had voted for President Trump in 2016, and half of white Christians from mainline denominations had done the same. Given the ongoing questions about his character—plus his administration's policies, which seem to fly in the face of Christian values—we thought that some percentage of the president's support from religiously minded voters could be peeled away. In a close congressional election, just a couple of percentage points from Christian voters could make all the difference. The best way, in my mind, to impede the progress of the Trump administration was to flip the House of Representatives to the Democrats, thus giving some much-needed checks and balances. We thought movable Christian voters could end up being instrumental in doing so.

I had coffee with my friend Stu and explained to him what I was doing and what Vote Common Good was trying to accomplish. He shook his head kindly and said, "You, my friend, are the patron saint of lost causes." I laughed and wondered if he was right.

The Vote Common Good tour started in Bethlehem, Pennsylvania. We spent the afternoon setting up the stage and a hundred chairs in a park in Bethlehem's town square. A storm was threatening to come through and rain on us, and we worried that the threat of bad weather would keep people away. Thankfully the rain held off, and as evening arrived, so did a bunch of people. I greeted our candidate, Susan Wild, when she arrived. Congresswoman Barbara Lee was campaigning with Susan that day and came as well. I was excited by the validation that having a sitting congresswoman speak at our first event would give our efforts. The program went well for our first time through. A few speakers took way too much time, but we adjusted on the fly, and it turned out okay. The music and the energy carried us through the night. Before she left, Congresswoman Lee said to me, "Robb, I feel like I've been to church tonight."

I thought to myself, *Good things start in Bethlehem.*

Over the next five weeks, we made our way across the country. Each day, we would stop in a congressional district, get set up, and greet the people who came. At some events, we had hundreds of people, but most were smaller—a few dozen or so. We always hoped for bigger crowds, but what we found was that the people who did show up were excited to be there. Often, we would hear from them that they were people of faith who were also progressive in their politics. Many would say that they thought they were all alone and had found at our events the tribe for which they had been looking. Even more than the impact on the people who attended, our stops were positive experiences for the candidates we were supporting.

Over and over again, they would tell me how encouraged they were by our speakers and musicians and how thankful they were that there was a progressive group doing outreach to white evangelicals.

Living on a bus for more than a month was a crazy experience. We had cramped quarters. Our bunks were small, and I often joked that I felt like I was sleeping in a coffin as we barreled down the highway. I was amazed that despite being far outside of our comfort zones with people who didn't know each other well initially, there weren't any personality conflicts. We spent the hours on the road talking and laughing and becoming family.

Somewhere in Virginia, we started to smell something foul. The stench of rotten eggs filled the bus. As it turned out, the batteries that ran the refrigerator and the air conditioning in the back of the bus were going bad. It made for a few really unpleasant days, but we were able to endure it with grace, knowing that what we were trying to accomplish on the tour was more important than any temporary inconvenience we would face.

With each event we held, we perfected our program. Doug developed a great opening that contrasted the rhetoric of the Trump administration and its policies with the teachings of Jesus. He had a litany he would run through with the cadence of an old-fashioned preacher, saying things like, "You have heard it said that we should separate families at the border, but I say unto you that whatever God has brought together, no one should ever separate." It was a moving way to get the crowds engaged.

Various pastors and speakers joined us for parts of the tour. Michael Waters, a pastor from Dallas, spoke with a passionate clarity and freshness that never ceased to move me. I told my kids later that I felt like I was on a bus and sharing a stage with the next Martin Luther King Jr.

I also grew to love Christy Berghoef, an author and speaker from Holland, Michigan. Each night, she would talk about how she was a mother who got involved in our efforts not just for her own children but for all of the children in our country who need someone to speak up for them.

Personally, I was excited to meet Frank Schaeffer when he joined us. Frank's dad, Francis Schaeffer, had been one of the founders of the Religious Right. In high school and college, I had read his books. They had so impacted me that Vanessa and I once had a dog named Schaeffer. Frank, like me, had gone through a faith shift that radically altered his perspective on politics. Whenever he spoke, he didn't mince any words, condemning the Trump administration with a fiery eloquence.

I also loved getting to know an artist named Genesis Be, a queer woman of color from Mississippi. She had gotten some press the year before for protesting the Confederate flag and knew firsthand what it was like to put herself in the public eye to demand justice in our country. At our event in Dallas, she performed for the first time a poem she had written called "Mississippi Is a Microcosm of America." Her words called out white supremacy and bigotry. When she finished, the crowd stood and applauded for several minutes. Genesis handed the microphone to me, and I thought, *How am I ever going to be able to follow that?*

Whenever I spoke, I knew that part of my role in the program was to create a space for Republicans and former Republicans to feel represented in their opposition to the Trump administration. I would joke with the audience that things had grown so crazy in American politics that here I was, a Republican, traveling the country campaigning for Democrats. I would tell the story of how I had run for Congress and how I learned that small things could make a big difference. I encouraged people to do the small things they could, like donating to, volunteering for, and most importantly, voting for our Vote Common Good candidates.

I had gone home for a weekend and missed part of the travels across West Texas, New Mexico, and into Southern California. I rejoined the group for our event on behalf of Katie Porter in Irvine, California. I started my talk that night by telling a story that Vanessa had shared with me on the phone earlier in the day. When Vanessa took Whimsy, who was by then four years old, to preschool that Monday morning, she told her teacher that Whimsy might have a rough day because her dad had left on a trip.

"What's your dad doing, Whimsy?" her teacher asked.

Without missing a beat, Whimsy replied, "He's going to fight Donald Trump."

When I told the story, the crowd cheered. "My toddler gets it," I told them.

The last night of the tour was in Fresno, California, one week before Election Day. We were tired from the trip but were determined to bring our best effort to our final event. Earlier in the day, we had received word that a group of people affiliated with the Proud Boys were going to protest us. The Proud Boys are a neo-Nazi organization committed to white nationalism and support of President Trump. When a half dozen of them arrived, a weird energy came over our event. As we sang and spoke, they stood at the back and heckled us. They yelled out responses to the things we said. More than anything, I felt bad for the people who had come to experience the Vote Common Good tour, only to be caught, literally, between our stage and these vocal protesters. I had never been heckled like this before when I spoke but was able to make it through my talk without being thrown off track by them.

When Genesis Be took the stage, we all held our breath. How would they respond to her? She took the microphone and mentioned the protesters in the back. She said that she had learned over the years that what our country needs is greater understanding and dialog. She then invited the leader of the Proud Boys to join her on stage. She handed him the microphone and gave him a few minutes to share his perspective. When he finished, all they could do was listen respectfully to her poem. Genesis showed us all how graciously acknowledging the presence of bigotry and hatred can diffuse it. It was a holy moment.

I got home from the tour in time to watch Election Day results. I was closely following the eleven races involving my Brand New Congress brothers and sisters who had made it to the general election. In the end, one of them was elected to the House of Representatives: Alexandria Ocasio-Cortez. I could not think of a better person to carry the banner of independent, progressive policy than her. She famously said that for one of us to make it through to Congress, hundreds of us would have to try. I was proud to be one of the ones who helped clear the path for her.

Sixteen of the candidates we had supported on the Vote Common Good tour made it to Washington too. The exit polling showed that 75 percent of white evangelicals had cast their ballot for Republicans in the midterm elections. That's still a huge number, but it was six percentage points lower than President Trump had received. I couldn't help but think that we had helped to move the needle, especially in some of the congressional races that were decided by only thousands, or even hundreds, of votes.

I had bought into a couple of big, crazy ideas that if we each did whatever small thing we could, it might make a big difference. And it had.

During the Vote Common Good tour, the music was led by Reverend Vince Anderson from Brooklyn, New York. In his signature raspy voice, Reverend Vince sings what he calls "dirty gospel." Each night of the tour, he performed a particular song he had written. And each night of the tour, it brought me to tears.

The song starts by describing how times are tough and it's easy to feel alone. Discouragement can set in. It seems like no one is listening, like no one cares. Our prayers become stale. Every word he sang described emotions I had during my campaign, in the aftermath of coming to grips with my loss, and when staring up the huge mountain of trying to get Christians to vote differently than they had in the past.

Reverend Vince would pause, letting the reality of the pain hang in the air—and then he would begin again with a refrain that he repeated over and over, building to a triumphant crescendo.

Please, don't give up because we need you now.
 We need you now.
Please, don't give up because we need you now.
 We need you now.
Please, don't give up because we need you now.
 We need you now.

I ran for Congress because someone needed to challenge the political establishment in my state and give people the choice and voice they deserve to have. I went on the Vote Common Good tour because religious people need to be reminded that the example and teachings of Jesus call us to care for others above ourselves. But there is still so much work to do. That's why we can't give up. We need you now.

Acknowledgments

During the campaign, I joked often that if I won, there would come a day sometime in the future when Vanessa would be upset with me that I had to be in Washington, DC, when she needed me at home. I planned on replying, "You can't blame me. This was all your idea." She didn't find this joke very funny. The truth is, this *was* all her idea. And it would have been impossible without her encouragement, wisdom, and love. I don't know who I would be or where I would be without her.

Two groups of people shared me with Arkansas's Third Congressional District during the campaign: my kids and Vintage Fellowship. I hope Matt, Calvin, Charleigh, and Whimsy know that I ran for them. And I hope the folks at Vintage know how grateful I am for the freedom they gave me to pursue a crazy idea.

I barely have words for how much Scott Ramsey has meant to me over the past couple of years. He went from friend to campaign manager and then back to friend. I couldn't have done any of this without him. Nor could I have done it without the people, too numerous to list, who donated to and volunteered for my campaign. I also want to thank a couple of friends who buoyed me along the way: Aaron Marshall and Mike Papacoda.

If it weren't for the amazing people at Brand New Congress, I never would have run for Congress. Thanks to Cory Archibald, Zeynab Day, Isra Allison, Saikat Chakrabarti, Corbin Trent, Haley Zink, Patric Taylor, Sam Briggs, Alexandra Rojas, Nasim Thompson, Zack Exley, Nicky Osborne, Ginny Bateman, Jennifer Craig, and a host of others.

Thanks to the entire Brand New Congress slate of candidates for blazing a whole new trail in American politics, especially the OG-BNC candidates who became my family: Alexandria Ocasio-Cortez, Chardo Richardson, Paula Jean Swearengin, Sarah Smith, Cori Bush, Michael Hepburn, Anthony Clark, Adrienne Bell, and Amy Vilela.

I never would have imagined that spending a month on a bus with a group of people could be so rewarding. I'm forever indebted to the Vote Common Good team for getting me back in the game: Doug Pagitt, Christy Berghoef, Samir Selmanovic, Rod Colburn, Brian McLaren, Tim Gilman, Michael Toy, Brandon Pfieffer, Frank Schaeffer, David Riordan, Mark Scandrette, Genesis Be, John and Jennifer Pavlovitz, Ben Corey, Jacqui Lewis, Michael Waters, Reverend Vince Anderson, Meah Pace, and more.

Thanks, finally, to the team at Westminster John Knox, especially Jessica Miller Kelley.

Notes

1. Francis Fukuyama, *Identity* (New York: Farrar, Straus, and Giroux, 2018), 6–7.
2. Brené Brown, *Dare to Lead* (New York: Random House, 2018).
3. Theodore Roosevelt, "Citizenship in a Republic" (speech, University of Paris, France, April 23, 1910).
4. Frederika Schouten, "The $5 Billion Election: How the 2018 Midterms became the Most Expensive in History," *CNN*, October 30, 2018, https://www.cnn.com/2018/10/30/politics/midterm-spending-smashes-records/index.html.
5. @NateBell4Ar (Nate Bell), "Fewer people would file primary challenges against incumbents if the fees were higher," Twitter, January 23, 2018, 9:13 p.m.
6. Rachael Bade and Sarah Ferris, "Arkansas Rep. Womack Likely Next House Budget Chairman," *Politico*, January 1, 2018, https://www.politico.com/story/2018/01/08/house-budget-chair-womack-black-328602.

CPSIA information can be obtained
at www.ICGtesting.com
Printed in the USA
FSHW010712220120
66200FS

9 780664 266219